Siri™
FOR
DUMMIES®

Siri™ FOR DUMMIES®

by Marc Saltzman

WILEY

John Wiley & Sons, Inc.

Siri™ For Dummies®

Published by
John Wiley & Sons, Inc.
111 River Street
Hoboken, NJ 07030-5774

www.wiley.com

Copyright © 2013 by John Wiley & Sons, Inc., Hoboken, New Jersey

Published by John Wiley & Sons, Inc., Hoboken, New Jersey

Published simultaneously in Canada

For general information on our other products and services, please contact our Customer Care Department within the U.S. at 877-762-2974, outside the U.S. at 317-572-3993, or fax 317-572-4002.

For technical support, please visit www.wiley.com/techsupport.

Wiley publishes in a variety of print and electronic formats and by print-on-demand. Some material included with standard print versions of this book may not be included in e-books or in print-on-demand. If this book refers to media such as a CD or DVD that is not included in the version you purchased, you may download this material at http://booksupport.wiley.com. For more information about Wiley products, visit www.wiley.com.

Library of Congress Control Number: 2012949803

ISBN 978-1-118-50881-7 (pbk); ISBN 978-1-118-54979-7 (ebk); ISBN 978-1-118-52698-9 (ebk); ISBN 978-1-118-54986-5 (ebk)

Manufactured in the United States of America

10 9 8 7 6 5 4 3 2 1

WILEY

About the Author

Marc Saltzman is a prolific journalist, author, and TV/radio personality specializing in consumer electronics, Internet trends, and interactive entertainment.

While *Siri For Dummies* is his first book for John Wiley & Sons, Inc., Marc has authored 15 books since 1996, covering topics such as video games, apps, mobility, and movies.

Along with his syndicated column with Gannett, Marc currently contributes to nearly 50 high-profile publications and online resources in North America, including *USA Today,* AARP, MSN, Yahoo!, *Costco Connection,* Common Sense Media, *Toronto Star,* Postmedia, Media Planet, and Sympatico. Marc hosts a number of video segments, including "Games and Gadgets" (a weekly spot on CNN) and "Gear Guide" (seen at Cineplex movie theaters and sister chains across Canada) and is a regular guest on CNN International, Daily Buzz, and CTV's Canada AM. Marc also hosts "Tech Talk," a syndicated radio spot across Canada. Follow Marc on Twitter (@marc_saltzman) and Facebook (www.facebook.com/marc.saltzman).

Dedication

This book is dedicated to my beautiful wife, Kellie, and my three awesome kids: Maya, Jacob, and Ethan. Thanks for letting me talk, joke, and argue with Siri — and for not calling the people with the white jackets to take me away.

Author's Acknowledgments

Allow me to take this opportunity to thank all the fine folks at John Wiley & Sons, Inc., for their knowledge (hardly *Dummies*), professionalism, and support. I'd also like to acknowledge the overworked yet often underappreciated public relations team at Apple, Inc.

Publisher's Acknowledgments

We're proud of this book; please send us your comments at http://dummies.custhelp.com. For other comments, please contact our Customer Care Department within the U.S. at 877-762-2974, outside the U.S. at 317-572-3993, or fax 317-572-4002.

Some of the people who helped bring this book to market include the following:

Acquisitions and Editorial

Project Editor: Pat O'Brien

Acquisitions Editor: Kyle Looper

Copy Editor: Beth E. Taylor

Technical Editor: Dennis R. Cohen

Editorial Manager: Kevin Kirschner

Editorial Assistant: Leslie Saxman

Sr. Editorial Assistant: Cherie Case

Cover Photo: © iStockphoto.com / Cary Westfall

Composition Services

Project Coordinator: Patrick Redmond

Layout and Graphics: Carrie A. Cesavice, Joyce Haughey, Corrie Niehaus, Christin Swinford

Proofreaders: Tricia Liebig, Lauren Mandelbaum

Indexer: Potomac Indexing, LLC

Publishing and Editorial for Technology Dummies

Richard Swadley, Vice President and Executive Group Publisher

Andy Cummings, Vice President and Publisher

Mary Bednarek, Executive Acquisitions Director

Mary C. Corder, Editorial Director

Publishing for Consumer Dummies

Kathleen Nebenhaus, Vice President and Executive Publisher

Composition Services

Debbie Stailey, Director of Composition Services

Contents at a Glance

Table of Contents

Introduction

. . . .

I'm thrilled to present you with *Siri For Dummies,* your definitive guide to unlocking the power of your favorite Apple gadget's voice-activated personal assistant.

Throughout these chapters, you find out how to take full advantage of Siri's awesome abilities — in a language you can understand. Yes, you can put away your geek-to-English dictionary, because you won't need it here.

Siri For Dummies covers all the things you can do on the iPhone 4S, iPhone 5, iPad (third- and fourth-generation, and iPad mini), or fifth-generation iPod touch — via your voice — ranging from productivity and connectivity features to information, calculation, and navigation. And of course, you see examples of the various responses you can expect through Siri.

About This Book

This book was meant to be read in any order. Sure, you can flip through it from beginning to end if you prefer a more linear read, starting with the introduction on what Siri is, its history, and how to use this remarkable tool. Alternatively, you can jump from chapter to chapter if one topic interests you more than another.

Each chapter can stand on its own, so you won't miss anything by reading out of order. (Aren't you a rebel!)

Of course, individual chapters focus on something specific Siri can do — such as transcribing your e-mails or finding a good Italian restaurant — with clear, step-by-step instructions on how to get the best results from your voice commands.

Because Siri is so versatile, you can often ask or instruct Siri to perform tasks in different ways than I've highlighted — not to mention the fact that you just might get a different response. The idea here is that you can use this book as a loose guide if you feel like experimenting with Siri's abilities or stick to the same phrasing as I used. It's really your call.

I also suggest ways to get what you need from Siri in the shortest number of steps, but you may prefer a more back-and-forth exchange with Siri if you're in the mood for a conversation. Hey, we all get bored or lonely at times; Siri can keep you company with small talk, stories, and cheeky comebacks to your requests.

Just as sections of this book are divided by individual task, there are a few subtopics within each chapter. For example, Chapter 6 is about how Siri can get you information you may need — but this chapter is broken up into definitions, fast facts, mathematical equations, stock and currency info, and voice-driven web searches. You get the idea.

In some cases, I cross-reference subjects with topics from other chapters when relevant, but you can ignore them if you like.

How to Use This Book

Consider *Siri For Dummies* a reference book. Therefore, you can start by thumbing through specific topics in the Table of Contents and then go to a particular chapter that interests you.

Although the book is meant to be informative, the tone is conversational. The only exception is the step-by-step instructions on performing the tasks in question. That is, when talking with friends in person I don't typically say things like, "Step 1 is to press such and such; Step 2 is to say this and that," and so on — but a *For Dummies* book helps by outlining the necessary steps required to perform actions.

Keep in mind that you'll probably benefit most from this book if you keep your iPhone, iPad, or iPod touch on hand while reading. That way, you can try out all of Siri's features on the spot.

What You Can Safely Ignore

When you come across a section within a chapter that contains the steps you need to take to get something done, you can disregard all text accompanying each step (the text that isn't in **bold**) if you're tight on time or don't want to read through more material. I won't be offended, really. Take what you need and ignore the rest.

As much as possible, I've also added various tips and tricks to getting the most out of Siri, along with a handful of optional "didya know?" tidbits. For example, Siri wasn't designed to let you update Twitter or Facebook using your voice, but I discovered a smart way around it.

But you don't need to wade through these factoids or ancillary abilities of Siri if you prefer to stick to the basics. Most of these extra paragraphs are labeled with Technical Stuff or Tip icons (see the "Icons Used in This Book" section). Then again, you may be more interested in these "sides" than the main course. (I'm sometimes like that when I visit my favorite deli.)

If you're more interested in finding out how Siri can help you remain productive when you do all the serious things you need to do on a day-to-day basis, you can also safely ignore Chapter 8, which focuses on fun and quirky things you can ask or say to Siri.

Also note that there are a lot of screen captures in this book. After all, *Siri For Dummies* is all about what you can say to your iPhone, iPad, or iPod touch, and what Siri will do, say, or display in response. Therefore, I want to show you as much visual information as possible, whether you have your smartphone or tablet nearby or not.

Foolish Assumptions

I'll make only two major assumptions: You own an iPhone 4S, iPhone 5, newer iPad, iPad mini, or iPod touch, and want to know how to get the most out of Siri.

When I write about speaking into your iPad, I'm referring to all Siri-supported models (the third- and fourth-generation 9.7-inch iPad and the 7.9-inch iPad mini) unless otherwise specified.

By the time you read this book, however, Siri might be a feature in other Apple products — such as the fifth-generation iPad, iPhone 6, and maybe even Mac-based computers or television products. So although I focus exclusively on the two latest iPhones and new iPads (including iPad mini), expect to see Siri expand to other products over the coming months and years.

On that note, throughout this book you'll see when Siri tasks are tailored to a specific Apple product, such as making calls on an iPhone instead of an iPad or iPod touch. I'll call them out to you ahead of time, though.

And as I make clear in the very next chapter, this is just the beginning of Siri. This voice-activated personal assistant will expand its abilities over time, too, so don't assume this is all Siri can do! The best, as they say, is yet to come. But this book covers everything you need to know right now.

Siri isn't available as a download for iPhones that came out before iPhone 4S, nor can it be used on the first two iPad models or older iPod touch. That is, you might be the proud owner of an iPhone 4 or second-generation iPad, but despite a few hacks you might read about online, there's no official Siri for these devices. Plus, you may have already sampled the Voice Control feature on previous iPhones or iPod touches, which let you control your music with your voice. This is also folded into Siri, but is just a fraction of what your new personal assistant can do.

Icons Used in This Book

The following icons are placed in the margins of the book's pages to point out stuff you may or may not want to read.

This icon warns you of geeky descriptions or explanations you may want to pass on — but don't expect a lot of these throughout this easy-to-read handbook.

This icon offers suggestions to enhancing your experience. Most are tied to the topic at hand, while others are more general in nature.

This icon reminds you of important information related to Siri. This info may have been covered previously in the book, but I thought it would be a good idea to refresh your memory.

Siri can be a powerful tool to getting information or getting things done, but this icon alerts you to important considerations when using Siri — including health, safety, or security concerns.

Where to Go from Here

If you've never used an Apple iOS product — perhaps you purchased this book in anticipation of buying one or receiving the phone, tablet, or media player as a gift — become familiar with the basic features of your device before having Siri perform tasks for you.

For example, you may try to interact with the Calendar app — with your fingertips — before turning to Siri to help you out. You not only gain a better understanding of what Siri is doing for you, but also gain a deeper appreciation of how Siri can speed up and simplify these tasks!

Occasionally, we have updates to our technology books. If this book does have any technical updates, they will be posted at dummies.com/go/sirifordummiesupdates.

That's it. As you can see, you don't need much to begin reading *Siri For Dummies* — just a desire to save time and aggravation while using your iPhone, iPad, or iPod touch. And as you find out in the final chapter, a sense of humor doesn't hurt either.

Chapter 1

Getting to Know Siri

Congratulations! You're now the owner of the most definitive guide to Siri on the planet.

This easy-to-read *For Dummies* title will teach you everything you need to know about Siri — and then some. Be prepared to master all of Siri's amazing features, at your own pace, so you can get a lot more out of your beloved iPhone, iPad (and iPad mini), or iPod touch. But first, a few words about my introduction to Siri, what Siri is exactly, and a bit of history.

As a longtime technology reviewer, I firmly believe Siri (pronounced *SEAR-ree*) is the start of something very special, and it was love at first sight — er, speech.

Here I am, sitting in the crowd at Apple headquarters in Cupertino, California, on October 4, 2011. The exclusive press event is called "Let's Talk iPhone," and like many other journalists and analysts in the room, I was expecting Apple CEO Tim Cook to take the wraps off the iPhone 5.

When the iPhone 4S was initially debuted, you could sense the initial disappointment among the attendees — after all, there were so many rumors leading up to the event that it seemed inevitable that a dramatically new smartphone would be unveiled that day.

But that letdown feeling completely vanished the moment Siri was introduced. Forget the iPhone 4S's faster processor, better camera, built-in support for the iOS 5 operating system and Apple's iCloud — the service that wirelessly synchronizes all your content between devices — it was Siri that truly held the magic that the late, great Steve Jobs often spoke of. (You may recall Jobs, Apple's visionary leader, passed away the following day, on October 5, at age 56.)

I knew right then and there, while at the Apple campus, that Siri would usher in a new and exciting way to interact with our mobile devices. I was so blown away by Siri that I e-mailed my book contacts on the spot, because I just had to be part of this revolutionary technology — and explaining to others how to best use Siri seemed like a fitting role given my effort to translate "geek speak into street speak" in my articles and TV and radio appearances.

If you've been following Apple happenings, then you're aware the iPhone 5 (finally) debuted nearly one year later on September 12, 2012 along with the availability of the new operating system that powered it: iOS 6.

With the new iOS 6 platform came a host of new Siri features (woo hoo!), including support for the third-generation ("new") iPad; a new Maps app and turn-by-turn GPS navigation; the ability to post directly to Facebook and Twitter; more movie, restaurant, and sports functionality; the ability to open any app using your voice; and much more. A new, fifth-generation iPod touch was unveiled at the same time, also with support for Siri.

Siri also became more international at this time, with support for Canadian French and English; Italian; Spanish (for Spain, Mexico, and the United States); Swiss Italian, French, and German; Mandarin for Taiwan; Cantonese for Hong Kong; and Mandarin and Cantonese for mainland China.

Siri might be exclusive to the latest iPhones, iPad, and iPod touch at the time of this writing, but it will likely play a major role in all Apple products going forward and hey, perhaps including Macs and Apple TV, too.

So What Is Siri, Anyway?

Siri can best be described as a personal assistant that resides on your iPhone 4S, iPhone 5, third- and fourth-generation iPad (including iPad mini), and iPod touch — all controlled by your voice instead of your fingertips.

In other words, Siri was built for talking rather than typing. And it goes both ways. Just as you can talk to your Apple device to perform a range of tasks (employing speech-to-text translation), you can also hear Siri's human-like voice talk back at you (text-to-speech technology).

Aha, so that's why "Let's Talk iPhone" was the name for Apple's iPhone 4S unveiling — because that marked the official debut for Siri, too.

 Think of Siri as being both software and a service, because all of your questions and commands are instantly uploaded to Siri's secure servers, and the appropriate actions and responses are sent back down to the iPhone, iPad, or iPod touch.

Apple doesn't often pull back the curtain on its technology, but here's how the company explains how Siri works on its FAQs (Frequently Asked Questions) page:

Siri uses the processing power of the dual-core A5 chip in iPhone 4S [the FAQs page has yet to be updated for iPhone 5, the new iPads, and iPod touch], and it uses 3G, 4G, or Wi-Fi networks to communicate rapidly with Apple's data centers. So it can quickly understand what you say and what you're asking for, then quickly return a response.

Using your voice, Siri can help you perform a number of tasks on your iGadget much faster than if you typed them. Such tasks include

- ✔ Sending e-mails and text messages
- ✔ Finding specific messages in your inbox
- ✔ Having your texts read to you — and you can reply verbally, too, and your words are transcribed back into text
- ✔ Using the Wolfram | Alpha database to quickly find useful information, such as dictionary definitions, mathematical equations, measurement conversions, or even fast facts and pop culture references
- ✔ Searching the web for anything and everything, including info and media (such as photos and videos)
- ✔ Posting updates to Facebook and Twitter
- ✔ Opening any app simply by asking Siri to perform the task for you
- ✔ Adding and accessing calendar appointments, alarms, timers, and reminders (Figure 1-1 shows an example of Siri doing just that)
- ✔ Making and accessing notes
- ✔ Getting directions from point A to point B — including audio-based directions you can listen to while driving — by using the GPS radio in the iPhone or iPad
- ✔ Finding businesses nearby — including directions on getting there — be it gas stations, banks, or restaurants; many businesses are also displayed by rating

✔ Making phone calls and FaceTime video calls

✔ Getting real-time information on weather, stock quotes, sports scores, movie reviews, and much more

✔ Booking dinner reservations through OpenTable simply by asking Siri

✔ Accessing music and podcasts using your voice, including the ability to control audio playback

Whew! And that's just the start. To get a taste of what Siri can do, be sure to watch the official Apple video on Siri at `www.apple.com/iphone/features/siri.html`.

Figure 1-1: Go ahead and give Siri a task, such as a reminder about an important date.

In fact, did you know Siri is still currently in *beta,* meaning Apple is still tweaking the software and service? That's right; as awesome as Siri is, it's not a final product. You can just imagine where Siri will go in the coming months and years.

Unlike other speech-to-text technology, including those offered by other smartphones, Siri works on the operating system level and knows which app to open based on your request. (Most other smartphone solutions require you to first open an app before you speak.) Using advanced artificial intelligence (AI), Siri makes connections based on your relationships, uses humor to make you smile, and is eager to learn more about your world and how to make your life easier to manage.

It's interesting that, just as Apple brought the mouse to the mainstream in 1984, changing the way we used keyboard-centric personal computers, they changed the game again by bringing a comfortable touch interface to the masses in the 2000s with the iPod, iPhone, and iPad. Now, Apple is making technological history yet again by bringing a speech-based user interface to the masses — arguably the most intuitive way to interact with computers to date.

And as we saw with Captain Kirk aboard the U.S.S. Enterprise in *Star Trek,* talking with computers and getting a humanlike response is the future. Let's just hope the computers don't turn on us like they did in *2001: A Space Odyssey, I, Robot,* or *The Terminator.*

Spend just a few minutes with Siri and you'll no doubt fall for its charm.

A Bit o' Background

Before I get into setting up Siri, you may be interested to learn just a tad about its history.

Siri is the result of more than 40 years of research funded by DARPA (the Defense Advanced Research Projects Agency). Much of the work has been carried out at the SRI International Artificial Intelligence Center, founded in 1966. (SRI, for those not in the know, stands for Stanford Research Institute.)

Fast-forward to 2007, when the company Siri (named, obviously enough, after SRI, the place of its birth) was founded by Dag Kittlaus, Adam Cheyer, and Tom Gruber, along with Norman Winarsky from SRI International's venture group. After a couple of successful rounds of financing, the company released an iOS app for Siri, with plans to make it available for BlackBerry and Android devices, too.

That's right: Seasoned iPhone users might recall Siri was a down-loadable app at the iTunes App Store a couple of years ago. The company was acquired by Apple Inc. in April 2010, and the app was pulled from the App Store — because folks at Apple had more ambitious plans for its future.

The official release date for Siri as an exclusive iPhone 4S feature began on October 15, 2011 in the United States.

The first major Siri update came nearly one year later with the launch of the iOS 6 operating system for Apple portable devices, which also added Siri to the latest iPad and iPod touch.

Also benefitting from speech-recognition technology licensed from Nuance (of Dragon NaturallySpeaking fame), Siri is also integrated with services such as Yelp, OpenTable, Google Maps, Taxi Magic, and MovieTickets.com, to name a few.

Setting Up Siri

Okay, before you dive into Siri's many features — covered in depth from Chapters 2 through 8 — here's a quick primer on setting up Siri properly.

First things first: Siri is already functional in all new iPhone 4S and iPhone 5 smartphones, and fifth-generation iPod touch (2012) so you don't need to download anything to get going. When you turn on the iPhone or iPod touch for the first time, you're prompted to set up a few things, such as enabling location information and using Siri, so be sure to choose Yes to these options. If you own the new (third-generation) iPad, which debuted in the spring of 2012, you must download the new iOS 6 update to add Siri functionality to the tablet.

By the way, you can always access Siri settings in the Settings area of your Apple device (tap Settings⇨General⇨Siri) if you need to make some changes. Figure 1-2 shows you the kinds of settings you can change for Siri.

Figure 1-2: Siri will open up your Calendar and add your requested appointment.

The first time you set up Siri, you're prompted to select the language you prefer. Your options are English (United States), English (Australia), English (United Kingdom), French, and German. (See Figure 1-3.)

Figure 1-3: It's important to select what language you need Siri to speak (and listen for).

But this isn't just so Siri can speak in a language you understand — it's also to let your new personal assistant better understand you. For example, someone from the United States or Canada will say "Call mom" differently than an English-speaking person from the United Kingdom or Australia. One might sound more like "Coll mum" or "Cull mam," and so on.

Sure, Americans have various accents, too — there are definitely subtle differences between those from Long Island, Boston, Dallas, or Minneapolis, for example — but American English can be vastly different from the English spoken in London or Sydney. So be sure to choose the correct language from the list or you may have some difficulties understanding Siri — and vice-versa.

It's also important to note Siri has a female voice in the United States, but that may not be the case with other countries (such as the United Kingdom, where Siri has a male voice).

For this reason, I usually refer to Siri as "it" for the majority of this book to keep it universal, but I do refer to Siri as a "she" from time to time, especially in the last chapter, which focuses on all the fun things you can say to Siri and things "she" will say back.

Okay, so I've covered the importance of choosing the right Siri voice from the list of available options, based on what language you speak and where you live.

Here are some other choices you have for Siri settings:

✔ **Voice Feedback:** You can select whether you'd like to always hear Siri talk to you through the iPhone, iPad, or iPod touch speaker (which might be heard by those nearby) or only when using a hands-free option, such as a Bluetooth headset. If you simply want to read Siri's responses instead of hearing them, select "Hands-free Only" and don't use a hands-free product.

✔ **My Info:** Here's where you'd want to list your name and contact information. You can tell Siri to call you something else, if you like (for example, a nickname), but this area points to your info in Contacts. For example, you can tell Siri, "Take me home," but she'll need to know where "home" is.

✔ **Raise to Speak:** The last option you have when it comes to using Siri is whether you want to set it up so that you always have to press and hold the Home button to speak to Siri, or if you'd like to also enable the Raise to Speak option, which automatically lets you talk to Siri whenever you raise your iPhone to your ear — meaning you don't have to press the Home button. Note: This isn't an option for iPad or iPod touch, but feel free to hold the tablet to your ear to make your friends laugh.

Because the Raise to Speak option isn't going to be everyone's choice, I'm going to assume for the rest of this book that you aren't using that particular feature when I provide instruction on using Siri. I always start each task with the standard "Press and hold the Home button" line, but if you choose to use the Raise to Speak option, you can ignore that bit and simply raise the iPhone to your ear instead.

The only other option you have to worry about for Siri is in the Passcode section (Settings⇨General). You can choose to use Siri even if your phone is locked (and requires a four-digit PIN) or you might opt to always force yourself to unlock your phone before you can use Siri. The advantage to using Siri when locked is you'll get your information faster — because you don't have to type in a code first to unlock the phone. On the flipside, allowing Siri to be used without unlocking the phone means if you lose your iPhone, iPad, or iPod touch (or if it's stolen), someone can potentially access information on your phone by asking Siri the right questions. It's your call, but remember this is an option that comes with pros and cons.

Talking to Siri

To talk to Siri, you simply press down on the Home button (that small circle at the bottom of your iPhone, iPad, or iPod touch), wait until you hear a short chime that sounds like two quick beeps, and then talk away.

 You'll also see a purple-tinged microphone icon on the lower portion of the screen. You'll know that Siri is listening to you speak because you'll see a lighted ring rotate around the microphone icon. (Figure 1-4 gives you an idea of what I mean, even if I can't re-create the rotating ring business.)

When you ask Siri a question — such as, "What's the weather like in Seattle tomorrow?" — you can stop talking after you're done and you'll hear a beep to confirm Siri is now processing your request.

Alternatively, you can tap the microphone icon when you're done speaking, which might be a bit faster than Siri waiting for silence to begin the request.

The next thing you'll see is your words spoken to Siri, in bold, near the top of your device's screen. This confirms to you that Siri understands what you're saying or asking.

If you make a mistake while asking Siri a question (maybe you accidentally said the wrong person's name to text) or perhaps Siri didn't hear you clearly, you can tap the microphone icon to let Siri know you want to cancel the request. After a second or two, you can tap it again and start over. You'll hear the familiar tone and see the ring rotate around the microphone icon to confirm Siri is listening for your new request.

Figure 1-4: Get used to seeing that little purple microphone.
This means you're chatting with Siri.

The final thing you'll see is when Siri performs your desired action. Siri might open up a map, an e-mail message, calendar entry, or restaurant listing. Depending on the task, Siri might also speak to you with the information you seek. With the weather, for example, you'll see and hear the answer, but if it's a dictionary definition or numerical equation, Siri might say something like, "Here you go" or "This might answer your question" and show you the information on the screen.

Because all requests to Siri are uploaded to a server, it's not unheard of for the server to be temporarily inaccessible — but it doesn't happen very often. Siri will apologize to you and ask that you please try again later. A problem with Siri *isn't* an indication that there's a problem with your phone, tablet, or iPod touch, so don't fret. The outage is usually only a couple of minutes (if that), but it's something you should be aware of.

Keeping the lines of communication open

This section gets into how you can up your success rate when it comes to using Siri, which comes down to making sure it understands what you're saying so that it can come back with quick and accurate results:

- ✔ You need to have a wireless Internet connection to perform all tasks — even if it's a local task such as asking Siri to jot down a shopping list in your Notes app. Whether it's a cellular signal you're using (make sure you see a few bars on the top-left of your phone) or Wi-Fi (a wireless network), you'll need decent reception to get quick results from Siri. This is critical.

- ✔ Speak clearly — I know this can be difficult to be conscious of — but the less you mumble and more you articulate your words, the better Siri works. Don't worry; Siri is remarkably keen on picking up what you say (and even what you mean) so you don't need to speak like a robot. Just be aware you'll get better results with clearer speech.

- ✔ A lot of background noise isn't great for Siri, as it might not be able to pick up what you're saying very well. The quieter the environment, the better Siri can understand your instructions. This might be tough if you're in a crowded restaurant, driving with the window open, or walking down a busy street, of course, so you might need to speak a little louder and closer to the iPhone, iPad, or iPod touch microphone.

Hands down, Siri is the most exciting thing to happen to Apple's portable products — but be aware that this new technology uses up quite a bit of data to function. As a result, make sure you have a good data plan with your cellular provider so you don't go over your monthly allowance. (You'll likely get a warning if you get close.) Also, using Siri can affect battery performance of the iPhone, iPad, or iPod touch; therefore, you may need to charge up your device every evening. Some "power users" — if you can pardon the pun — invest in a battery pack that keeps your iGadget topped up all day long.

You can call me Al

Siri refers to you by your name — sometimes you'll see it written, and in some cases you might hear it spoken aloud by Siri. But did you know that you can change what Siri calls you? That's right, at any time you can tell Siri what you'd prefer to be called, and your request will be granted.

Here's what to do:

1. **Press and hold the Home button.**

   The little chime you hear means Siri is listening for your request.

2. **Tell Siri something like, "Call me Dude."**

   Siri will then say something like, "Okay, from now on I will call you Dude." You can tap Yes or Cancel. See Figure 1-5 for what you'd see on your iPhone screen.

Figure 1-5: You can ask Siri to call you something else, if you like.

Going forward, when Siri addresses you personally, you'll see and hear "Dude" instead of your real name, as you'll see in Figure 1-6. Need I mention that it's okay to have fun with Siri? It feels good.

Figure 1-6: Change your name to whatever you like, and Siri will call you that — until told otherwise.

As you'll soon find out with the help of this fine book, you can also tell Siri who the important people are in your life, such as, "My mom is Honey" (yes, that's my mom's real name!), "My dad is Stan," and "My wife is Kellie," and Siri remembers all of this. Now you can say things like, "Text my dad," "E-mail my mom," "Call my wife," and so on. Go ahead and tell Siri important relationships, as well as key dates, such as birthdays and anniversaries, too.

Okay, now that you've nailed the basics, you're ready to tackle *Siri For Dummies* in any order you like. Feel free to jump around or simply swipe to the next page to begin with Chapter 2, which is all about getting organized — including using Siri for calendars, reminders, notes, alarms, timers, and more. Much, much more.

"The Beta Test Initiation"

Siri has already been immortalized in pop culture, thanks to a tribute by the cast of *The Big Bang Theory*. Starring four socially awkward friends — two physicists, an aerospace engineer, and an astrophysicist — the hit CBS sitcom devoted an episode to the female-sounding personal assistant in its January 26, 2012 episode.

The character Rajesh Koothrappali (played by Kunal Nayyar), who is unable to talk to women unless he's inebriated, romantically bonds with Siri and even comes face to face with the woman behind the voice. It's a hilarious episode (number 101 in the TV series), so be sure to watch it!

Chapter 2

Using Siri to Organize Your Life

*I*n Chapter 1, you find out about some of the amazing things Siri can do for you — at a high level. Time now to take a deeper dive into some of the ways Siri can help you stay organized and informed, wherever life takes you.

Specifically, Siri can seriously speed up common — and often mundane — tasks, such as adding entries to a calendar, setting a reminder to do something, making notes, and setting alarms.

Menial tasks that often take multiple steps when typing can be performed in mere seconds — with great accuracy — when you get to use your voice.

And with the latest Siri update, you can now have Siri open apps for you, which can save you time from trying to find them among your many dozens or hundreds of apps.

Siri is your savior, in other words, and so without further ado, I cover how to take advantage of your voice-activated personal assistant to get more done in less time.

Keeping a Calendar

Whether you rely on your smartphone personally or professionally (or, in all likelihood, a little bit of both), your trusty handheld device can definitely help you stay organized while on the go.

After all, unlike a paper day timer (if you remember those!), your smartphone can alert you to important meetings, wirelessly synchronize this information with other devices, and also let you easily search for entries by keyword.

Siri goes one step further by making it drop-dead simple to add or access calendar entries — without having to stop to manually type in all the information.

 To minimize redundancy, be sure to take advantage of Apple's iCloud service, which wirelessly synchronizes all your information and content between multiple devices (up to 5GB for free). Your calendar entries automatically sync with your personal computer or other iOS device (such as an iPod touch). When you add or edit an entry on your iOS device or computer, all devices are updated over the Internet. To set up calendar entries with iCloud, go to Settings on your iPhone, iPad, or iPod touch, tap iCloud, and swipe to turn on Calendars (underneath Contacts).

Adding new calendar entries

Adding a new calendar appointment using Siri is a breeze. Follow these steps:

1. **Press and hold the Home button.**

   The little chime you hear means that Siri is listening for your instructions.

2. **Tell Siri about a calendar appointment you want to make.**

   For example, say, "Remember to call Auntie Terry-Lynn at 5 p.m. tomorrow" or "Set up a meeting about the sales report at 9 a.m. Thursday." (Figure 2-1 shows what a Meet-Wife-at-Noon request to Siri looks like.)

3. **Confirm or cancel the appointment.**

   Say "Cancel" or "Yes" — or tap Cancel or Confirm — to either cancel or confirm the appointment.

Siri might warn you that your proposed appointment overlaps with an existing one. (See Figure 2-2.) Or Siri might ask you to confirm the person you want the meeting with (this could happen if you say, "John," for example, and there are nine people named John in your Contacts). If you say or tap Cancel, Siri will stamp a red CANCELED notification across the screen, and you might see some words like "All right, I'll leave it off your calendar."

Siri isn't too picky: You can ask Siri to set up an appointment in a number of different ways. You can say, "Add calendar entry," "New appointment with *person*," "Set up a meeting," or "Meet with *person*," to name a few examples.

Figure 2-1: Siri will open up your Calendar and add your requested appointment.

Figure 2-2: If there's a calendar appointment overlap, Siri warns you about it.

Adding a new calendar entry — with location information

Along with the date and time, you can also use Siri to set a location for your appointment:

1. **Press and hold the Home button.**

2. **Give Siri a calendar-related command.**

   Say something like, "Schedule a sales meeting tomorrow at 9 a.m. in the boardroom."

3. **Review what Siri is showing you.**

Preview the calendar entry — time, subject, and place — before accepting the appointment. The location for the meeting displays underneath the subject, as shown in Figure 2-3.

After Siri shows you the confirmed calendar appointment, you can tap the screen and it'll open the Calendar app for you to add or edit details, if desired. Or maybe someone walked into the room and you'd rather type discreetly than talk out loud. Simply tap the Edit button, and you can make all kinds of alterations, including when the meeting starts and ends, the time zone, alerts and repeats, related web-sites, and notes. You can also delete the event from here, too. Just be aware that you can edit your spoken calendar entry with typed words, if you like.

Figure 2-3: In this calendar entry, you see where the meeting is to be held ("boardroom").

Making changes to calendar appointments

Siri can do more than just create a new appointment. You can also use Siri to review and change calendar appointments.

The following are a few examples of what you can say to Siri to change or cancel appointments when you're on the run. Using Siri is much faster than doing these tasks yourself!

✔ **Change an appointment.** You can instruct Siri to do this for you. For example, tell Siri, "Move my 3:30 p.m. meeting to 4:30 p.m." (See Figure 2-4.) You can also say, "Reschedule my appointment at 3:30 p.m. to next Tuesday at 1:30 p.m."

Figure 2-4: Changing an existing appointment to another time is as easy as pie.

✔ **Cancel a calendar appointment.** Tell Siri something like, "Cancel my 12 p.m. lunch meeting with Julie." Or if you want to feel important — like those rich CEOs in the movies — you can even say something like, "Cancel my 1 o'clock!," and Siri will ask you if you want to cancel the calendar appointment for that time. Have your people call my people.

✔ **Add someone to an existing calendar appointment.** For example, tell Siri, "Add Mary Smith to my meeting at 3:30 p.m." (Figure 2-5 shows you how Siri complies with your request.)

Figure 2-5: Based on your instructions, Siri adds Mary Smith to your appointment with Mike Jones.

You can use Siri even when your iPhone, iPad, or iPod touch is locked — but only if you want to. That is, by default, you can pull your device right out of your jacket pocket or purse and press and hold the Home button to give Siri some instructions (or if you're wearing a Bluetooth headset, press and hold the button to activate Siri). This can save you a step as you need not unlock the phone first. But if you prefer, you can turn off this feature in the Passcode Lock settings (tap Settings⇨General⇨Passcode Lock⇨Siri).

Reviewing calendar appointments

Siri can also help you quickly review your calendar appointments. The following bullet list highlights a few examples of what you can ask Siri and what you see and hear in return:

- ✔ **"What does my day look like?"**

  Siri shows you today's calendar entries.

- ✔ **"When is my next meeting?"**

  Siri tells and shows you the time for your next appointment.

- ✔ **"What do I have on Friday?" (See Figure 2-6.)**

  Siri displays all calendar entries for a given date.

- ✔ **"When am I meeting with Julie?"**

  Siri says and displays the time for your next appointment.

- ✔ **"Where is my meeting with Steven?"**

  Siri tells you the location for the relevant appointment and shows you the calendar entry, too.

Figure 2-6: Ask Siri what's on tap and you can see your calendar appointments.

Setting Reminders

Apple added a handy Reminders app to your iOS device, found on your Home screen (the front page of all your apps). As the name suggests, this app lets you create and view quite a few reminders — without having to add them to your calendar.

This pocket-sized to-do list, if you will, makes it easy to set or view reminders. For example, when viewing reminders, there are multiple ways to organize everything you have to do — be it by date, priority, location, or any custom-made list you want to create (such as Family Stuff, Work Notes, and so on). And of course, the Reminders app notifies you when you should do that thing you need to do.

Siri makes using Reminders a lot easier as it takes just a few seconds to instruct Siri to add a reminder to your to-do list.

The next sections explain how to get going.

Starting a reminder

If you'd like Siri to remind you to do something in the future, take out your Apple device and try the following operation:

1. **Press and hold the Home button.**

   The familiar chime you hear lets you know that Siri is ready for action.

2. **Tell Siri what you'd like to do.**

   Speak into your iPhone, iPad, or iPod touch with a command such as, "Remind me to buy milk, bread, and eggs today at 4 p.m." or you can say something like, "Remember to thank John for the present."

3. **Glance at your screen to review your reminder. Or listen to Siri's confirmation.**

4. **Assuming everything looks good to you, say or tap "Yes" to create the reminder. (If something isn't quite right, say, "Cancel," to cancel the reminder.)**

   Figure 2-7 shows you what a reminder confirmation from Siri looks like.

Because it takes only a quick Siri request to set up a reminder, you might be tempted to do this while driving. But even a minor distraction could cause an accident, so resist using Siri until you've parked the car.

Figure 2-7: Here's what a typical reminder confirmation looks like — after you've approved it.

Telling Siri when to remind you

If you tell Siri to remind you about something but don't specify a time or date, you'll be asked to do so on the spot. Neat, huh? This is how the exchange looks with Siri:

1. **Press and hold the Home button.**

   You know that Siri is ready for instructions when you hear the familiar chime.

2. **Tell Siri what to remind you of.**

   For example, say, "Remind me to call mom."

3. **When Siri prompts you to specify a date and/or time, tell Siri when you'd like to be reminded of whatever you stated needed reminding.**

   Figure 2-8 shows you what a reminder on your iPhone looks like.

Here's something fun to try with Siri, which may amuse the kids or grandkids. Ask Siri to remind you of something *way* in the future. For example, I asked Siri to remind me to tie my shoes in 10,000 years, and I was asked if it should be placed in my calendar then. (Won't our shoes automatically tie themselves then?) See Figure 2-9. Too funny!

Figure 2-8: If you forget to tell Siri when to be reminded, you'll be asked to set a date and time.

Figure 2-9: Wow — that's thorough. Siri had better remind me to tie my shoes in the year 12,012.

Setting a location for your reminder

One of the coolest things about using Siri is you can ask to be reminded to do tasks by location, too. Because the iPhone and iPad are location-aware (thanks to its GPS, cellular, or Wi-Fi technologies), you can instruct Siri to remind you about something when you leave or arrive at a particular location. (However, for optimal performance, use cellular and GPS connectivity for location-based reminders.)

Here's a quick step-by-step on using Siri to remind you about a task when you leave somewhere:

1. **Press and hold the Home button.**

   The short beeping sound you hear indicates that Siri is ready.

2. **Tell Siri to remind you about something — but at the end say, "when I leave here."**

   For example, say, "Remind me to buy flowers and wine when I leave here." (See Figure 2-10.) Another example: "Remind me to take an umbrella when I leave" (no "here" is necessary).

Figure 2-10: Siri displays your reminder request, with your geographical location info at the bottom of the reminder.

3. **Preview the reminder and if it's good, say "Yes" or "OK," or tap "Confirm."**

   You'll see your address at the bottom of the reminder. (As you can see, I took the liberty of covering up my address for privacy reasons!) When you leave this address, your iPhone or iPad will remind you to pick up flowers and wine.

Now, say you want to be reminded about something when you arrive at a particular location? Here's how to use Siri to perform this handy task:

1. **Press and hold the Home button.**

   Siri tells you it's time to speak your request with the familiar chime.

2. **Tell Siri to remind you about something but add the words "when I get to *destination*."**

   For example, you can say, "Remind me to FaceTime with Mary Smith when I get home" or "Remind me to talk to John about the contract renewal when I get to the office."

3. **Siri sets the reminder — and location — and asks that you confirm the details.**

   If Siri doesn't know your home or business address, you'll be asked to fill in this information in your Contacts (and Siri will open it up for you), as shown in Figure 2-11.

You can also combine a date with a location! For example, you can tell Siri something like, "Remind me to make a doctor's appointment Monday morning when I get to the office."

Figure 2-11: Siri didn't know my home address, so I was prompted to give it (just once).

Previewing your reminders

You can also ask Siri to preview your reminders. She won't read them to you verbally, but she will tell you if you have any you should know about and display them on the screen.

To preview your reminders, follow these steps:

1. **Press and hold the Home button.**

   Hearing the Siri chime is your cue to begin speaking.

2. **Ask Siri if you have any reminders.**

You can ask it in different ways, but it might be easiest to ask, "Do I have any reminders today?" Or you can ask "Do I have any reminders tomorrow?" or "Do I have any reminders next week?"

Siri displays whatever reminders you have listed in the Reminders app for a given date or location.

As shown in Figure 2-12, you can ask Siri to show you reminders by location, too (in this case "at home").

Figure 2-12: You can ask Siri to show you a list of uncompleted reminders.

Although Siri can quickly show you reminders for today, it's even faster to slide your finger down from the top of the screen to open the Notifications list. Part of this screen includes upcoming reminders for the day. Also, remember that you can also turn on

Reminders in the iCloud service, meaning all reminders will be synched between your iPhone, iPad, iPod touch, Mac, and PC. To set this up on your iOS device, tap Settings⇨iCloud⇨Reminders.

Now this is worth an LOL. In the spring of 2012, if anyone asked Siri, "What is the best smartphone ever?," the answer would be the Nokia Lumia 900, based on the Microsoft Windows Phone operating system. (See Figure 2-13.) Siri provided this information because the Nokia smartphone was the highest rated, at that time, according to its Wolfram | Alpha database (more on this later in the book). As you would expect, this was egg on Apple's face — by saying the competition's platform is better than the iPhone platform — and so now, when you ask Siri this question, you get a very different result (see Figure 2-14).

Figure 2-13: This is what you saw in the spring of 2012, when you asked your iPhone to tell you the name of the best smartphone.

Figure 2-14: Hmm, did Siri change its mind overnight? You see this reply if you ask the same question. As you can see, I asked twice.

Taking Notes

As with most smartphones and tablets, the iPhone, iPad, and iPod touch ship with a Notes app — all decked out to look like yellow, lined pieces of paper — allowing you to jot your thoughts down whenever they pop into your head.

The Notes app isn't a full-blown word processor — for example, there are only three font styles to choose from — but it's an ideal tool to flesh out ideas and make lists and such. And with iCloud, Apple's handy way of synchronizing all of your digital info and media over the Internet (between supported devices), all your notes can be synched with all your devices, too.

You can, of course, manually tap to open the Notes application, start a new note, and begin typing — or you can be smart and have Siri do it for you.

You can use Siri to start a new note, add words to an existing note, and pull up notes based on keywords.

Creating a new note

Here's a look at the first task I mentioned, starting a new note:

1. **Press and hold the Home button.**

   You hear the familiar tone, which is your cue to begin talking.

2. **Instruct Siri to create a new note for you.**

   You can say something like, "Note that I spent $50 on the fantasy football pool," "Create a note called 'Buy these books for mom,'" or "Take a note to pick up that new Xbox 360 game for Steve."

   Siri opens up the Notes app, begins a new note with the name you've given it, and then shows you the note it just created for you. (See Figure 2-15 for an example of Siri's response when I ask her to create a note.) The first few words of your spoken note become the name for the note, but you can change that if you like.

You won't get a chance to accept or cancel the note Siri creates for you. If you don't want to keep the note, you'll need to manually open up the Notes app and remove it. You can't delete notes using Siri.

Take note that you can ask Siri to create a note in different ways, such as saying, "Make a note about *this,*" "Take a note about *that,*" or just "Note that I did *this and that.*"

Adding more to an existing note

If you've created a note on your iOS device and you want to add more to it, you can do so very easily with Siri's help. All you need to know is what the note is called (or as you'll see shortly, you can do a search by keyword), and you can add more text using your voice.

Here's how to get going:

1. **Press and hold the Home button.**

You know it's time to talk after you hear the familiar chime.

```
..ıl.. Bell 🔋          3:47 PM          ❋ ▭

  ❝ Make a note to buy a
    new memory card for
    mom's digital camera ❞

  Noted:

  ┌──────────────────────────────┐
  │ buy a new memory card for mom's │
  │ digital camera                  │
  └──────────────────────────────┘




              🎙
```

Figure 2-15: Siri can help create notes for you on the fly.

2. **Tell Siri something like, "Add cereal to Shopping List note."**

   Remember, the note you're adding the extra words to must already be in your Notes app. Remember, when you start a new note, the first few words will be the title for the note.

3. **Look at the screen to see the note — and what has just been added — and, assuming it's all good, you can put the phone away.**

   See Figure 2-16 for an example.

4. **(Optional) If you need to edit the entry, tap the message, and the Notes app opens.**

As you can see in Figure 2-16, Siri won't always capitalize proper nouns ("jobs" should be capitalized in "Steve Jobs"), so you can manually change this by tapping the screen — if it bothers you at all, that is.

Figure 2-16: Add more information to an existing note using Siri.

Finding notes

Your voice-activated personal assistant can also be used to find existing notes on your iPhone, iPad, or iPod touch.

Perhaps you're looking for that grocery list while standing in your local supermarket? Or maybe you want to add more detail to your million dollar idea?

Instead of manually scrolling through all your notes, you can ask Siri to show you all relevant notes by saying a keyword — or all your notes, if you prefer.

Here's a quick guide on what to ask Siri:

1. **Press and hold the Home button.**

   You can begin talking after you hear the short chime.

2. **Either ask Siri to display all your notes or ask her to look for one in particular.**

   Tell Siri, "Show me all my notes," and you'll see a list of them, from newest to oldest, as shown in Figure 2-17. Tap a note to open one up. Alternatively, ask Siri to look for a particular note by telling her something along the lines of, "Show me 'book' notes," which will have her call up all notes containing the word "book." (See Figure 2-18.)

Figure 2-17: Siri can show you all your notes, if you ask it to do so.

Figure 2-18: I asked Siri to show me all notes with the word *book* in them.

Setting Alarms, Clocks, and Timers

You can quickly set an alarm on any Siri-enabled iOS device by asking "her" to set it for you.

Before I show you how to do this (very) simple task, I want you to think of all the steps involved if you didn't use Siri. Say you want to be woken up tomorrow at 7 a.m. Without Siri, you'd have to open up your Clock app, tap on Alarm at the top of the screen, and then tap + to set a new alarm. Now you must select a time (for example, 7 a.m.) and tap Save. Geez, that's a drag, no?

With Siri, all you have to do is ask her to set an alarm at a given time. Two to three seconds at most, and you're done.

Setting an alarm

Here's the easiest way to set an alarm:

1. **Press and hold the Home button.**

   You can ask to set an alarm right after you hear the chime.

2. **Say what time you want the alarm to go off.**

   For example, say, "Wake me up at 7 a.m. tomorrow." (See Figure 2-19.) Siri will show you the alarm, based on your request.

Figure 2-19: In this case, the alarm was previously set and turned off, so Siri turned the alarm back on for me.

You can close this app if it's correct or swipe to turn it off if it's not.

Siri has additional alarm features that enable you to instruct Siri to do the following:

✔ **Want to take a nap?**

Tell Siri, "Wake me up in one hour."

✔ **Need to sleep in a little longer tomorrow?**

Instruct Siri to "Change my 7 a.m. alarm to 7:30 a.m."

✔ **Want to call in sick?**

Say, "Cancel my 7 a.m. alarm."

✔ **Want to remove the alarm notification altogether?**

Tell Siri, "Delete my 7 a.m. alarm."

Finding out what time it is

Siri can give you the time — locally or in another city altogether. Siri can also tell you today's date.

Want to call a colleague's mobile phone in Hong Kong but don't want to call too late or too early? Here's what to do:

1. **Press and hold the Home button.**

   You hear a chime, which means Siri is ready for you to ask her a question.

2. **Ask Siri what time is it in Hong Kong.**

   Within a second or two, you can see the exact time in Hong Kong. (See Figure 2-20 for an example.)

 You can ask Siri to tell you the date today or another day (for example, "What is the date this Friday?"). Or you can ask Siri a question like, "How many days until Christmas?" and you'll see a thorough response from Siri, as shown in Figure 2-21.

Figure 2-20: Siri shows you the current time in Hong Kong — and tells you that it's tomorrow's date, too.

Setting and adjusting timers

Finally, speaking of clocks and alarms, Siri can also be used to set a timer on your iPhone, iPad, or iPod touch.

Figure 2-21: I asked Siri to tell me how many more days until Christmas, and she broke it down for me.

Whether you want to know when to check the oven, leave the house to pick up the kids from a play date, or stop jogging around the neighborhood, you can easily set a timer using voice commands. It's as easy as this:

1. **Press and hold the Home button.**

   Listen for the chime and begin speaking.

2. **Instruct Siri to set a timer.**

   You can say the duration of the timer right away (see Figure 2-22) or say, "Set a timer," and Siri will ask you, "For how long?" However you set the duration, when that's done you'll see the timer start.

Figure 2-22: Don't let that roast burn in the oven! Siri can set a timer for you in a flash. All you have to do is ask.

3. Preview the timer information at a glance.

Tap the timer info if you want to

- Change when the timer ends.
- Change the kind of alarm that sounds (by default it's Marimba).
- Pause the timer.

For even more fun, try these other timer-related commands with Siri:

✔ **"Show the timer."**

✔ **"Pause the timer."**

✔ "Resume the timer."

✔ "Cancel the timer."

If the timer is already open on your portable device, you can simply say, "pause," "resume," or "cancel."

Opening Apps with Siri

One of the new Siri features introduced with the Apple iOS 6 platform is the ability to open up any app on your iPhone, iPad, or iPod touch by using your voice.

There are a couple of ways to open up your apps, based on your wording and what apps they are, but Siri will handle most apps with this simple request "Open [app]." That's it!

Here's an example:

1. **Press and hold the Home button.**

   You'll hear the familiar Siri chime, which means that Siri is ready for you.

2. **Tell Siri to open an app, such as "Open photos" or "Open iTunes U."**

   Within a second or so, the app you asked for will be open and ready for action.

Voice command

Many owners of iOS gadgets have many, many screens of apps on their iPhone, iPad, or iPod touch. Without voice commands, there are several ways to open the app you want:

✔ Flick around and try to find the app manually (which might be buried in a folder, too!).

✔ Swipe to the right on your Home screen (the first page of apps) and search for an app by typing in a keyword (such as "OpenTable" or "ShopSavvy" or "Readability").

✔ Reopen apps by double-tapping the Home button on the bottom of the device and scrolling through open (but background) apps on your device.

As you can see, none of these aforementioned scenarios are the most ideal because they can take some time to access what you want — especially flicking around and manually finding apps.

Thankfully, Apple now lets you open up any app on your iPhone, iPad, or iPod touch instantly by simply *asking* for it.

This task is performed faster if the app was recently opened (it's simply minimized in the background).

There's not much to illustrate here because Siri doesn't show you anything — other than your verbal request. See Figures 2-23 and 2-24 for an example of what this looks like. Siri does not give you a verbal confirmation for this task, by the way.

Figure 2-23: Siri confirms your request by showing what you asked on the screen, just before the task is performed.

Figure 2-24: A mere second or two later, you see the app open on your iPhone, iPad, or iPod touch. In this case, it's the entertainment app Sock Puppets. (Try it — you'll like it.)

You can also tell Siri to "Play" an app, such as a game. For example, you might say "Play Angry Birds." Usually, it works. But be aware that sometimes Siri might think you're looking for a song to play rather than an app — because she can do that, too (see Chapter 6). If this happens, Siri may say something like "Sorry, I couldn't find the song Angry Birds to play." Just to avoid aggravation, I recommend sticking with "Open," followed by the name of the app you want to open with your voice.

Chapter 3

Using Siri While on the Go

In This Chapter

▶ Finding out how Siri can give you accurate directions

▶ Using your voice to search for destinations, including points of interest (POIs) and landmarks in other cities

▶ Taking advantage of the new Apple Maps application, viewable in 3D, too

▶ Searching for nearby restaurants, stores, bank machines, and other businesses

▶ Having Siri tell you about the weather — locally and around the globe

*W*ithout question, Siri is the most exciting feature in Apple's iOS products — and because these smartphones, tablets, and media players were made for portability, you can bet that Siri can help you when you're out on the town. Or even in the countryside, for that matter.

Specifically, Siri is a fast and powerful way to discover the world around you. If you need turn-by-turn directions, want to find a new restaurant (also see the next chapter!), or simply want to know if you need an umbrella today, Siri can help you with all of these scenarios, and much more.

This chapter helps you unlock Siri's capabilities when you're out of your home and looking to roam.

Turning to Siri for Navigation

Because the iPhone and cellular-enabled iPads have built-in GPS technology, they can communicate with satellites that hover above the planet and help pinpoint your location on earth. When paired with the new Maps app on the device, you can use it to get where you need to go — simply by asking Siri to help.

Some iPads can't be used for GPS navigation. The sidebar shows you the ins and outs.

Introduced in the fall of 2012, the Apple iOS 6 operating system is the first to use the Apple Maps app instead of the Google Maps app used previously. This is a significant change, and if you want to get somewhere and search for local businesses by using your voice, then you'll love what's new here:

✔ Get voice-based, turn-by-turn directions — even from the Lock screen

✔ Ask Siri to repeat herself, if need be (maybe your spouse asked you a question, and you didn't hear Siri)

✔ Find out where gas stations are along the way, what the traffic is like, and how long until you get there

You can even ask Siri something kids have asked from the backseat since the invention of the automobile:

"Are we there yet?"

Although not quite as powerful as standalone GPS navigation units (or downloadable GPS apps for iPhone like TomTom or Garmin, for that matter), the new Maps app and Siri integration is in a word, awesome:

✔ For the first time in the history of iPhone, you get free turn-based navigation with both visual and audio cues to help you on the road, on foot, or while taking transit.

✔ Add Siri, and you can use your voice to get directions to a particular location and, within seconds you'll see where to go, how to get there, and how long it might take.

The next sections show you a few ways to use Siri while on the go.

Using Siri to find an address

Unlike most GPS units, where you need to type in the state, city, and address of the place you want to go, your iPhone offers a voice-activated personal assistant to simplify this common task.

TECHNICAL STUFF

Can you get there from here?

Although all versions of iPhone have GPS navigation capabilities, only *cellular-enabled* iPads can be used as a GPS navigation device:

✔ Siri only works with the new (third-generation) iPad — at the time of writing this, anyway. Therefore, you need a 4G-enabled iPad (16GB, 32GB, or 64GB model) and active data service to get turn-by-turn directions on your tablet when on the go.

✔ Older iPads with 3G wireless connectivity can be used as a GPS navigation tool but not with Siri support.

✔ Though the latest iPod touch supports Siri (woo-hoo!), these portable media players have no GPS chips. You can still make business searches or view places in the Maps app via Wi-Fi connectivity.

Similarly, tablets that only have Wi-Fi don't have GPS navigation. All Wi-Fi iPads can launch the Maps app and show you directions to a location or search for businesses, but you won't be able to take it in the car for real-time directions.

To find a specific address:

1. **Press and hold the Home button.**

   Siri is ready for your instructions after the short chime.

2. **Tell Siri where you want to go by starting with "Take me to" or "Give me directions to," followed by the street address, city, and state.**

   You could, for example, say, "Take me to 1 Infinite Loop, Cupertino, California." (I bet you already knew that this address is in fact the world headquarters of Apple.)

   Figures 3-1 and 3-2 show you what Siri finds.

   As you can see, Siri opens up the Maps application, powered by Apple, and drops colored pushpins at your location and the final destination.

3. **Tap Start in the upper-right corner to begin the turn-by-turn directions.**

Figure 3-1: Siri confirms the address you want, before opening the Maps app.

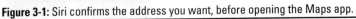

Figure 3-2: I'm pretty far away, but Siri's directions span across the entire United States and Canada.

Within a moment, Siri begins to give you audio instructions, such as "Head east down First Street toward Third Avenue. In 300 feet, turn left." You will also see visual instructions now, including a large green sign at the top of the screen with your first set of instructions (such as "Start on 1ˢᵗ Street, turn left in 300 feet"). You'll also notice a close-up map on the screen that shows your current location — you're the gray arrow — and nearby street names. See Figure 3-3.

Figure 3-3: Here's what the new Apple Maps app looks like when it's giving you directions.

Now you can start driving (or walking, cycling, or rollerblading) to your destination, and Siri will give you visual and audio instructions along the way.

 Want to see the overhead view of where Siri is taking you? While you're on the way to your destination, you can tap the screen anywhere and you'll see the word Overview in the top-right corner. Tap it to get that large map that shows where you're going. Now tap Resume in the same top-right corner of the screen to continue with the turn-by-turn instructions. Figure 3-4 shows an example.

Figure 3-4: Tap the screen to bring up this extra information, including a look at an overview of your travels, estimated time of arrival, distance to destination, and more.

When you tap the screen to bring up the Overview map, as shown in Figure 3-4, you'll also see additional details that could help you on the road:

- ✔ At the top of the screen, you can see the time and operating information about your device (battery life, carrier you're on, and wireless signal strength).

- ✔ Essential navigation information includes

    - ETA (estimated time of arrival) to your destination

    - Estimated time it takes to get there based on driving the speed limit

    - Number of miles away

You can tap End in the top left to finish your navigation, if you no longer need the help.

Because the new Maps app on the iPhone and iPad has voice-guided, turn-by-turn directions, there's no need to glance down at the phone or tablet while behind the wheel. Siri speaks loud and clear with its verbal instructions, so be sure not to look at the screen until you've parked. If you need some help hearing Siri — perhaps because your car is filled with noisy kids — wirelessly sync or dock your iPhone or iPad with your car stereo to hear the audio through the car speakers. Others might wear earbuds, but make sure it's not too loud because you may not be able to hear sirens from emergency services vehicles, such as ambulances, fire trucks, and police cruisers.

Whether you're mounting your iPhone in your vehicle or simply carrying it in your hand while on foot, you can choose to see the maps in either

- ✔ Vertical view (portrait). See Figure 3-5.
- ✔ Horizontal view (landscape). See Figure 3-6.

Figure 3-5: Do you enjoy holding your smartphone, tablet, or iPod touch vertically? Here's what the Maps application looks like.

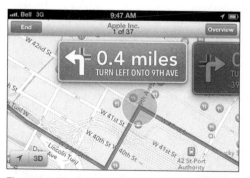

Figure 3-6: The horizontal (landscape) view of the Maps app on an iPhone.

Simply tilt and turn your device, and the maps give you the look you want.

After Siri starts giving you turn-by-turn directions, you'll notice the large and clear text (such as street names and distance information) and smooth animation that transitions from one set of instructions to the next. It's also fast and responsive — even if you throw in a last-minute stop for gas (see later in the chapter).

Apple's new Maps app offers other ways to get information. You might've noticed some tabs at the bottom of the screen — one says 3D, another has an arrow, and a third looks like a list:

✔ Tap the 3D button for an angled or *isometric* top-down view of your surrounding areas, so you can gauge the topography, and depending on the city, witness visually striking three-dimensional imagery of buildings and mountains as if you were there and seeing it with your own eyes. At any time, you can toggle between the normal 2D flat top-down view and the slightly angled 3D view.

✔ When tapped, this small arrow takes you back to your exact location by using your phone's location-aware technology, such as GPS, cellular, or Wi-Fi radios. This is a quick way to jump back to your current location when scrolling around on the map.

✔ Tap the icon that looks like a list (lines and dots) to bring up the text-based directions to your destination (as shown in Figure 3-7). Here you see an itemized view of your travels, in chronological order, including how long to travel down each road (for example, 0.3 miles or 410 feet). You also see which way you'll need to turn when done (indicated by a white arrow on a green background and Siri saying "sharp left" or "slight right"), name of the street, image of the freeway signs, and so on. This feature is handy as you might want to get an idea of your trip before you leave.

Your iPhone, iPad, or iPod touch were made for multitasking, so don't feel as though you can't do something else on your device while Siri is guiding you. Your friend can browse the web or read e-mail on your device while you're driving, no problem. Simply press the Home button and perform another task, and you'll still hear what you need. The glowing green bar at the top of the screen reminds you that the Maps app is still open and running. As you can see in Figure 3-8, you can tap the top of the iPhone or iPad to resume visual instructions.

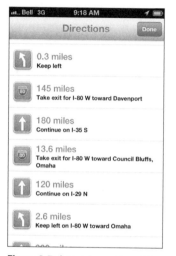

Figure 3-7: A text-based breakdown of your travels, turn-by-turn, toward your destination.

Figure 3-8: The Maps app is still open and running in the background (and you can still hear Siri).

Performing multiple tasks with the iPhone or iPad can take a toll on the battery as well as use up data toward your monthly limit.

Using Siri to give you directions between two addresses

When you need to plan travel or give someone directions that don't begin or end with your current location, Siri is at your service. For example, say that you're taking a road trip to New York City from Buffalo, New York and you're curious about getting to Washington, D.C. from your hotel in Manhattan. You can easily obtain directions.

To find a specific address, follow these steps:

1. **Press and hold the Home button.**

   Begin speaking after the short chime.

2. **Tell Siri where you want to get directions from and to.**

   For example, say "Take me to 1 Infinite Loop, Cupertino, California, from W Hotel, Times Square, New York." See Figure 3-9. Alternatively, using this same example, you can flip it around and say "Get me directions from W Hotel, Times Square, New York, to 1 Infinite Loop, Cupertino, California."

Figure 3-9: Ask and ye shall receive: Siri takes me to Apple headquarters from a hotel in Times Square in Manhattan.
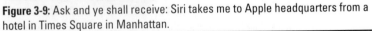

3. **If it looks good to you, tap the Start button on the top-right of the screen. See Figures 3-10 and 3-11.**

   Siri shows you the turn-by-turn instructions visually.

   There's no audio because Siri *knows* that you're not there, so you don't need that at that exact time. In fact, you can now flick to the left when you see the instructions — the large green and white sign with "200 Feet" at the top of the screen, being swiped away — and you'll see it start flipping through each set of instructions. Cool! See Figure 3-12.

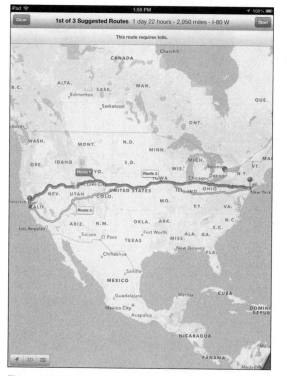

Figure 3-10: An overview of the entire trip — whether it's across the entire country (like this) or around the block.

As you can see in these images, Apple's Maps app is similar to Google Maps, which is the software used by Apple before switching to its own technology in the fall of 2012.

Figure 3-11: Now you can start the turn-by-turn navigation between two locations.

Figure 3-12: Flick to the left to scroll through all green instructions.

You can switch between various views, drop pushpins manually to flag an address or area you want to detour to, and also show traffic, if supported, in the city you're in. You can also print directions and map images to an AirPrint-enabled printer for a paper copy!

To change views and access this additional information, tap the page curl in the bottom right of the screen (shown in Figure 3-13). After you're there you'll see the various options for map views.

In Figure 3-14, you can see the different map options at your fingertips — such as one of three views, including standard map, satellite photography, or a hybrid of the two — as well as traffic information, printing options, and the ability to drop pushpins on the map.

Figure 3-13: Tap the page curl in the bottom right of the screen to open up a host of map options — just like Google Maps.

Figure 3-14: Tap one of three views to suit your taste, print directions, view traffic, or drop pushpins.

Because the Maps app stays open and running when you press the Home button on your iPhone, iPad, or iPod touch, be sure to properly close the app when you no longer need it — or else it could drain your battery or eat up your monthly data plan (excluding the iPod touch because no models use cellular technology). There are a couple of ways to properly close the Maps app:

✔ Tap the End tab inside the Maps app to end the navigation. But depending on what task is running inside the Maps app, you may or may not see the End tab. If that's the case, consider the next option.

✔ Follow these steps to properly close Maps — (or any iOS app you no longer want running):

 1. Double-tap the Home button from your home screen (where you see your apps).

 A multitasking bar appears at the bottom of the screen.

 2. Press and hold an open (but minimized) app, such as Maps.

 All the icons will start jiggling.

 3. Tap the small red minus badge on the Maps app to close it down.

Using Siri to find a location without an address

Siri isn't just for finding addresses you know; you can also ask Siri to take you to landmarks, attractions, and businesses.

For example, say you're in Orange County, California, and want to know how to get to Disneyland from there. You don't need to search for a specific address to the theme park in Anaheim — just let Siri know that you really want to see Mickey:

 1. **Press and hold the Home button.**

 2. **Begin speaking after the short chime.**

 Tell Siri, "Take me to Disneyland!" (as if you've just won the Super Bowl).

 Siri opens up the Maps application, figures out where you are based on the iPhone or iPad GPS, and shows you the way to Disneyland.

3. Pack up the kids and head out the door.

You'll see visual directions to the park, either with a standard view (see Figure 3-15), satellite view, or hybrid of the two (shown in Figure 3-16). Simply tap the small Page Turn icon in the lower-right corner of the Maps screen to make your selection.

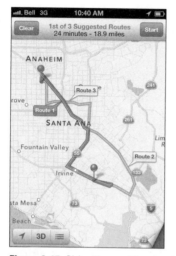

Figure 3-15: Siri will open Maps and show you the standard view to your destination.

Figure 3-16: Alternatively, you can view the map using a satellite or hybrid view. (The latter is shown here.)

The Maps app can show you alternate routes, where applicable, as you'll see here in Figure 3-17. You can also tap the bottom right of the screen (where it looks like a page turning) and then press the Traffic tab to see what the situation looks like on the roads at that time. This might sway you to take one route over another. Traffic near L.A.? Unheard of (cough)! See Figure 3-18.

Figure 3-17: In this scenario, you can choose from one of three routes.

Figure 3-18: The new Apple Maps app does a good job of warning you about congestion.

Apple is working to integrate Siri in next-generation vehicles. Called *Eyes Free,* car manufacturers will add a dedicated button for the driver to press on the steering wheel to initiate Siri. Among the companies looking to integrate Siri by late 2013 (in alphabetical order): Audi, BMW, Chrysler, Jaguar, GM, Honda, Land Rover, Mercedes, and Toyota. Ford already has a voice-activated technology in many of its cars, Sync, in partnership with Microsoft.

When looking at a map, you could place two fingers on the iPhone, iPad, or iPod touch screen and turn the map around, from left to right or right to left, to get a different view. You can also pinch in or pull out on your fingers to zoom in and out in real-time, too. It's cool and handy. See Figures 3-19, 3-20, 3-21, and 3-22 for examples of multiple satellite views of the same area in Miami Beach. Check out the compass at the top right, with the red side of the needle pointing north.

Figure 3-19: A top-down view of beautiful Miami Beach, Florida.

Asking Siri to see an address

One feature that many iPhone, iPad, or iPod touch users might not be aware of is the ability to see the address to where you want to travel. Sticking with the Apple Inc. headquarters as an example, you can ask Siri to show you what the campus looks like and you'll see it on your screen within seconds.

Figure 3-20: Use your fingertips to twist and turn the view, now facing east.

Figure 3-21: A zoomed-in look by swiping two fingers away from each other on the screen.

Figure 3-22: A higher-up view by swiping fingers away toward one another to zoom out. Note the compass in the top right, pointing north.

After all, you may want to get an idea of the street layout around the building, a nearby park, or other landmarks or details you can see from the overhead map. More on this in a moment.

To see what a location looks like:

1. **Press and hold the Home button.**

   The little chime you hear means Siri is listening for your instructions.

2. **Tell Siri about an address you'd like to see on the Maps application.**

   For example, say, "Siri, show me 1 Infinite Loop, Cupertino, California."

Siri does what you ask. (Hey, she's your loyal personal assistant, after all.)

The first view you'll see is of a standard top-down map view of the area, with 1 Infinite Loop front and center (see the pushpin in Figure 3-23).

Figure 3-23: Apple's campus looks like this in standard Map view.

3. **If you'd like, tap the screen to open up the Maps application and then tap the small Page Turn icon in the lower-right corner of the Maps screen to choose another view.**

   The hybrid view, which folds in satellite imagery, is kind of neat. See Figure 3-24.

You can also ask to see a city at a glance, from above, by simply saying the name of the city. See Figure 3-25, for an example with New Orleans:

✔ Tap the screen to open the navigation menu (shown in Figure 3-26), including your desired view (I chose hybrid for Figure 3-26) and 2D or 3D view.

✔ Tap the small blue and white arrow for more information including how far the city is from your location, directions there, and other options at the bottom of the screen (see Figure 3-27).

Figure 3-24: Tap the screen to open up the Maps app, allowing for more options.

Figure 3-25: Hey, it's the Big Easy! Just by asking Siri to show it to you.

Figure 3-26: Tap the map once to bring up the official Maps view for the city — in satellite, standard, or hybrid view.

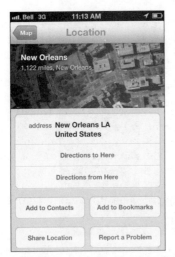

Figure 3-27: After you've tapped the small blue-and-white arrow beside the term *New Orleans,* you can see other information below it.

Apple says it plans to introduce *flyovers* in some cities. This feature lets you see major metro areas and its landmarks from the air with photorealistic, interactive 3D views. Figure 3-28 is the official photo with this feature.

Figure 3-28: Check out this flyover look at Sydney's famous opera house.

If you look at Figure 3-26, you may notice an arrow at the top left of the map, on a right angle. Tap it, and it lets you choose the start and end points of your travels. By default, the Start area is your current location, but you can tap that window and type a different starting address instead. Or tap the microphone tab beside the spacebar and say the address aloud. See Figure 3-29. You can also do this for the end address you want to tap to. Want to reverse the start and end addresses? Press the twisting arrow on the left of the address windows to swap the two addresses. The middle of the screen shows you the recent history of your travels in the Maps application. When you're done, tap the Route tab at the top right of the screen to begin the turn-by-turn directions.

You can tap to select directions by car, on foot, or by public transit (via third-party app) for more accurate directions based on your preferred mode of travel. See the top of Figure 3-29 for icons that represent car, foot, or transit. For example, on-foot directions differ from in-vehicle directions because you can walk any direction you like on a one-way street, cross through parks, and so on. Unlike the original Google Maps app, transit isn't yet supported natively on the new Apple Maps app — but is likely to show up in a future update.

Figure 3-29: Type or say the address you want to travel from and to. At the top of the screen are travel-mode icons: car, transit, or on foot.

When you're typing or talking to Siri with a destination to travel to, you will see a small address book logo at the top right of the map screen. Tapping this brings up the Contacts app. For example, if you want to drive to, say, your aunt's house, and already have her address in your Contacts, simply select her name, and the Maps app does the rest! You can also use your voice to do this from your home screen, if you like, as you will soon see in this chapter.

Canadians, rejoice! Updated in the fall of 2012, the latest Siri now supports maps, directions, and business searches in the Great White North. This support wasn't available in the first version of Siri. Canada and the United States are now fully supported, whether you want to find great sushi in Vancouver, how to get from Calgary to Denver, to the CN Tower in Toronto, or the Notre-Dame Basilica in Montreal.

Telling Siri to take you home

Had enough of where you are? Can't seem to figure out where you are? Realize you need to run home because you forgot to walk the dog? You can instruct Siri to take you home, wherever you are. It's as easy as asking.

You might need to tell Siri where "home" is if prompted to do so, but you'll need to do this only once:

1. **Press and hold the Home button.**

2. **After you hear the chime, simply tell Siri, "Take me home" or "How do I get home?"**

3. **Review what Siri is showing you.**

   Siri opens your Maps app and drops a pushpin on your home address.

4. **Tap the right arrow on the top right of the screen and follow the written and visual instructions for going home. (See Figure 3-30.)**

Figure 3-30: Even if you're in another state, you can get the fastest route home, thanks to Siri and the Maps app.

While you can tell Siri to take you home, you might not want to take advantage of this feature — especially if you don't make it a habit of locking your iPhone, iPad, or iPod touch. Why, you ask? If you lose your smartphone or tablet, a tech-savvy thief can ask Siri to "take me home" and know exactly where you live. Instead, perhaps you want to put your local shopping mall as your home address, as you can likely find your way home from there without any assistance. Just food for thought!

Telling Siri to direct you to someone in your Contacts list

Did you know that you can also ask Siri to take you to a friend or colleague's residence or workplace? You can say, "Take me to Mary Smith's house" or "Show me the way to mom's work." As long as you have the address of the person you're looking for in the Contacts app on your iDevice, Siri can help out.

Here's an example:

1. **Press and hold the Home button.**

2. **After you hear the chime, simply tell Siri to take you to someone in your Contacts list.**

   For example, say, "Take me to Tore Dietrich's office." (See Figure 3-31.)

   Siri will find the contact in your address book, find the specific address you requested, and open your Maps app to show you the address, as shown in Figure 3-32.

3. **When you're ready to go, tap the right-pointing arrow and start your journey.**

4. **Follow the directions to get to your destination.**

Figure 3-31: Tell Siri to take you to someone's address in your address book — work or home.

Figure 3-32: Siri opens Apple's Maps app and gives you directions.

A number of companies have provided information for the new Maps app experience, including

- ✔ TomTom, AND, and Increment P Corp (map data)
- ✔ Acxiom and Localeze (business listings)
- ✔ DMTI, Getchee, Waze, CoreLogic, LeadDog, and Intermap (maps and postal data)
- ✔ Yelp (reviews)

Using Siri for Location-Based Searches

Now take a look at how Siri can help you find establishments around your hometown — or even in another city.

For example, you can find a restaurant not just by name but also by type of food you're looking for. You can ask Siri to find a good place to eat based on what you're in the mood for. You'll see relevant restaurants listed by type of cuisine, proximity, and rating (thanks to the awesome Yelp service).

Although I cover this in much greater depth in the following chapter, I want to go over it a bit here, too, because it's tied to the new Maps app, too. But be sure to read Chapter 5 for a lot more on Siri's tasty restaurant-related features for iPhone, iPad, and iPod touch owners. Okay, here's an example of what you can do:

1. **Press and hold the Home button.**

   You'll hear the familiar Siri chime, which means you can ask her to find a restaurant.

2. **Instruct Siri where you to want to go or what type of food you feel like eating.**

   For example, tell Siri, "Find a good steak house near me," "Show me the best Italian food in New York," or "I'm in the mood for Indian cuisine." (See Figure 3-33 for an example.)

   Siri shows you relevant results within a couple of seconds, as shown in Figure 3-34.

   You usually receive good suggestions, but sometimes an incorrect cuisine is thrown in (seeing a BBQ joint when you ask for Italian, for example), the odd omission (such as missing the highest-rated restaurant), or recommendations for poorly rated restaurants.

Figure 3-33: When you ask Siri for good Japanese food, she sorts the results for you.

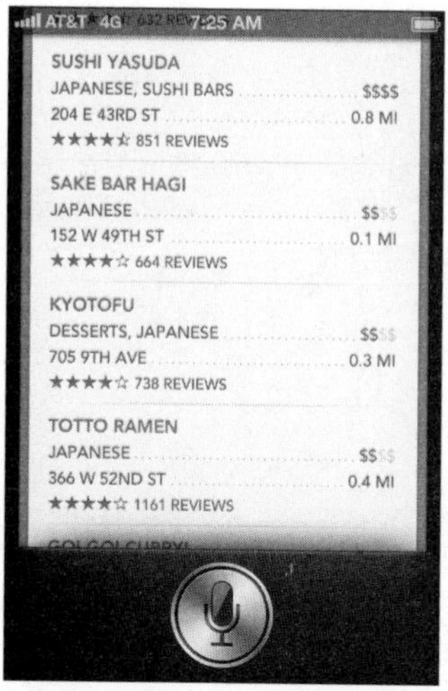

Figure 3-34: Flick upward on the results to see additional pages. Tap an entry for info and directions (if necessary).

3. **Peruse the listings and tap the one that interests you the most.**

   After you tap a desired restaurant, Siri opens up the Maps application to show you where it is. You'll see the name of the restaurant clearly on the map; tap it for more detail, such as the exact address or phone number. Or, if you like, choose to add the address to Contacts or to Map Bookmarks, or get directions to the place from where you are.

You can ask for a food or drink category (for example, "Find coffee near me") or be more specific ("Where is Starbucks?"). You can also ask Siri to search in different ways; Siri is amazingly versatile, so you can use language that's comfortable to you. You can even try slang like, "Show me the best burger joints in Atlanta." See Figure 3-35, where I asked Siri to find some Mexican restaurants in a city I was planning on visiting.

Siri's local searches aren't limited to only restaurants — but it's a fun place to start.

Figure 3-35: Siri lists many Mexican restaurants in Vancouver, all displayed by Yelp rating.

The following are a few other things you can ask or tell Siri, and you'll get a list of options, with navigation support:

✔ **"Find the nearest gas station."**

Driving on fumes? You can see a list of nearby stations to fill up your vehicle with fuel.

✔ **"Where is an ATM machine that's within walking distance?"**

Get turn-by-turn, on-foot directions to the closest ATM.

Siri often won't recommend an ATM inside of, say, a restaurant, or a Starbucks built into a hotel lobby. It's not perfect, but hopefully it will improve its accuracy over time.

✔ **"Siri, I feel sick."**

Your personal assistant shows you nearby clinics or hospitals.

✔ **"List the closest churches to me."**

Need to get a quick prayer in? If you like, be more specific (for example, include the words, "Catholic church" or ask for a "mosque" or "synagogue").

✔ **"What's playing at the movies?"**

Siri brings up movie listings at nearby theaters (see Chapter 5).

See Figures 3-36, 3-37, and 3-38 for examples of location-based searches.

Figure 3-36: Don't run out of gas! Just ask Siri where to fill up.

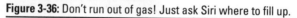

Figure 3-37: Traveling to a city? Siri can scope out what you want before you get there. And check out the iBooks plug! What a character Siri is.

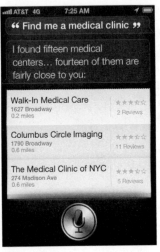

Figure 3-38: Ask Siri to list medical clinics, and she'll comply. Or say you're not feeling well.

What's the Weather Like? Ask Siri!

The final section in this chapter covers all the ways Siri can fill you in on the weather — not just today but in the near future, too. And not just in your local area but in another city altogether!

A simple question to Siri can yield the answers you seek. But of course, that doesn't mean that the answers will always be accurate (neither is your favorite TV weatherperson).

As long as you have your iPhone, iPad, or iPod touch handy and a voice to ask Siri a few questions, you can get a quickie weather forecast right on the spot.

Here's an example of the most basic way Siri can help with your weather forecasting:

1. **Press and hold the Home button.**

   You'll hear the familiar Siri chime, which means you can begin talking.

2. Ask Siri what the weather's like.

See Figure 3-39 for an example of what you can ask and how Siri responds. (Notice you also get a weeklong forecast!)

Siri shows you the current weather for your city within a couple of seconds.

Because the iPhone and iPad are location-aware (thanks to its GPS chip), you don't need to tell Siri what city you're in.

Figure 3-39: Siri responds when asked what it's like outside.

Because Siri is context-sensitive, you can ask for the weather in different ways — and you'll likely get the response you seek. You might ask if it's cold outside. Or ask Siri to tell you the temperature. See Figure 3-40 for yet another way to phrase it.

Okay, so say you want to know what the weather's like in another city — perhaps you're planning a trip there — and it's still a few days away? No worries, as Siri can give you the local weather forecast and weather for multiple places around the globe (up to five days in the future).

For example, you may want to ask Siri what the weather is supposed to be like in London, England, on this coming Saturday. Figure 3-41 shows you how Siri would respond to that question.

Figure 3-40: Ask and ye shall receive! Ask Siri if you need an umbrella (or say, "raincoat" and you might get a "yes").

Figure 3-41: Too bad the forecast isn't promising for this weekend in London.

Here are some other examples of what you can ask Siri, when it comes to the weather:

- ✔ **"How's the weather in Minneapolis right now?"**
- ✔ **"How hot will it be in Bangkok this weekend?"**
- ✔ **"What's the projected high for Montreal tomorrow?"**
- ✔ **"What's the forecast for tonight?"**
- ✔ **"Check the forecast for Washington, D.C., this week."**
- ✔ **"How windy is it outside?"**
- ✔ **"When is the sunrise tomorrow in Acapulco?**
- ✔ **"Will it rain in Dallas this week?"**
- ✔ **"Do I need a jacket tonight?"(See Figure 3-42.)**

Figure 3-42: Tonight's forecast — how did we ever live before Siri?

Chapter 4

Using Siri for Sports, Movies, and Restaurants (Oh, My!)

. . . .

In This Chapter

▶ Finding out sports scores to live games — and even past ones

▶ Reviewing schedules, player stats, and team rosters stats for many kinds of sports

▶ Asking Siri about movie show times near you, playing trailers, and looking up film facts

▶ Checking out movie ratings and reviews to current and past films

▶ Finding restaurants by location, cuisine, and price

. . . .

*A*pple updated Siri by adding more support for on-demand information and location-based services, including sports, movies, and restaurant information.

Sports fanatics, for example, can now take advantage of Siri's vast knowledge about teams, players, and leagues, as well as access real-time scores and schedules for sports such as football, baseball, basketball, hockey, and soccer.

ESPN, eat your heart out.

What's playing at a theater near you? Just ask Siri. Movies are now a big part of Siri. If you're on the fence about a flick, ask Siri to play a trailer or show you a review via Rotten Tomatoes (a popular website for movie reviews, trailers, and box office numbers). If you're interested in facts about a film, director, or star, just ask Siri. For example, you can ask "Who directed *The Godfather.*" Siri gives you the answer — Francis Ford Coppola.

Finally, this chapter is ideal for foodies, too. Oh sure, even first-generation Siri could recommend a good place for sushi, Mexican, or barbeque — as you read about in Chapter 3 — but now you can ask your digital assistant for suggestions based on your budget, reviews, or number of stars awarded by Yelp, the popular website for local business listings and ratings. And with OpenTable, why not use your voice to book a reservation? The future is here, and it's delicious.

Turning to Siri for Sports

Batter up, baseball fans. Hold on, hockey lovers. If you're into these sports — as well as football, soccer, or basketball — you'll no doubt find your new iPhone, iPad, or iPod touch an invaluable tool, all thanks to Siri.

Now it's possible to stay current with your favorite sport, team, and player, simply by asking for information.

With Siri and a partnership with Yahoo! Sports, you can ask about past, current, and upcoming matches, get stats to support an argument with a friend, or find out who's pitching in a home game you've scored tickets to.

Although Apple doesn't advertise this fact, did you know the new Siri can handle college ball, too? This includes college football and men's and women's college basketball. And it's not just Major League Soccer (MLS) that's supported for footie fans — how about French Ligue 1 or Dutch Eredivise? No problem.

Even if you're into other sports, just ask Siri about it and if the information isn't immediately accessible, Siri will do a web search for you. For example, I asked "Which country won the most medals at the 2012 Olympic Games?" and Siri's quick web results showed it was the United States with 104, followed by China at 88, and Great Britain with 65 medals.

But you'll be surprised just how much Siri knows without turning to Safari for a little help.

Here's how sports fans can use Siri to the fullest.

Using Siri for live sports scores

Siri is great for finding scores to live or past games. That way, you can save yourself the time of web browsing to get the information, launching a sports app, or (gulp) turning on AM radio for the news.

To find out a live sports score:

1. **Press and hold the Home button.**

   Siri is ready for your instructions after the short chime.

2. **Ask Siri the score of a game being played.**

   You could, for example, ask "What's the score of the L.A. Galaxy game?" or "Who's winning the Chicago Blackhawks game?" You don't have to say the full team's name; therefore, asking how the "Yankees" are doing instead of the "New York Yankees," is usually fine — unless more than one sports team has the same name, of course.

   Figures 4-1 and 4-2 show you what Siri delivers.

   As the information is being displayed — in real-time, no less — Siri will also say something like "Okay, sports fans, let's have a look" or "Here you go."

3. **If you want to go back to the home screen, simply press the Home button again.**

Figure 4-1: Ask and ye shall receive — asking about a live baseball game.

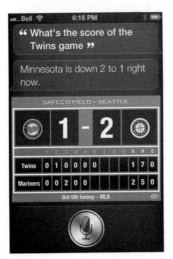

Figure 4-2: Siri delivered this live update when I asked how the Twins were doing.

If there isn't a live game based on the team you asked for, Siri will tell you the final score of the last game played by the team. She might say something like "The Blue Jays lost a close one to the Rangers yesterday; the final score was 2 to 1."

Don't just close the score after you get what you need:

- As you can see in Figure 4-3, the screen shows additional information, such as

  - The arena and city in which the game was played

  - Each team's official logo

  - The score per quarter, inning, or period

  If it was a playoff game, the results of the entire match are included (such as, "Oklahoma City Wins Series 4-1.").

- For many games, if you have the free Yahoo! Sportacular app installed, you can tap the small Y! logo in the bottom-right corner to launch the app and see even more information.

Figure 4-3: With a basketball game as an example, Siri shows you more info than just the score.

Using Siri for previously played games

What's that — you forgot to find out how well your favorite team did yesterday? Just ask Siri.

Just as you can ask about live games, Siri can tell you how various teams and players did from a past game or season.

Using Major League Soccer as an example, here's what to do:

1. **Press and hold the Home button.**

   Wait a moment for the short chime.

2. **Begin speaking after the tone.**

   Ask Siri, "How was DC United's last game?" See Figure 4-4 for what this looks like. You can also ask, "How did the White Sox do?" or "Did the Penguins win?"

   Siri then displays the information you seek, by giving you the date, score, and teams. It's that easy!

Figure 4-4: Siri displays the score of a previously played soccer game. Just ask for your favorite team.

Siri also tells you the results of the last known game played based on the team you ask about, even if it was the previous season's final match. Or, if you ask for current scores, she might tell you something like "I believe we're just waiting for the season to get underway."

Asking Siri to tell you about two teams

Maybe you don't want to know about the last game a team played, but are curious about a final score between two teams.

For example, you can ask, "What was the score the last time the Red Sox played the Yankees?" Maybe these teams are meeting up again, and you're curious about the outcome of the last time they met up.

To see what this looks like

1. **Press and hold the Home button.**

   The little chime you hear means that Siri is listening for your instructions.

2. **Ask Siri to tell you the score between two teams.**

   Inquire about any two teams, and Siri will show you the answer. See Figure 4-5.

3. **Look at the screen for the information you seek.**

   Siri won't verbally tell you the scores, but they are displayed on the iOS screen.

Figure 4-5: How does the last game between these two rival teams stack up? Ask Siri, and you'll get the answer.

You can also ask Siri to give you information about an entire league. For example, you can ask "Show me the college football scores from yesterday" or "Siri, show me all the hockey scores from last week," and you'll see the entire schedule with a summary of scores within this timeframe — and whether it was a home or away game. See Figure 4-6.

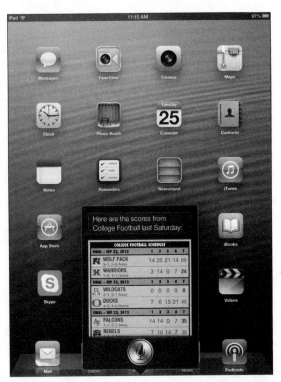

Figure 4-6: Get a quick glance at an entire league by asking for all scores.

Asking for more sports info from Siri

Siri can do so much more for sports fans.

What's that? You want some examples, you say. Well, okay, then. How about this:

> ✔ You can also ask Siri what time a game starts. For example, ask "What time is the New York Rangers game?" Siri might say "The Rangers – Blue Jays game starts at 1:07 p.m."

You can also see what TV networks carry the game and each team's stats for playing at home and on the road. You can also ask something like "When do the L.A. Lakers play next?," "Show me the baseball schedule?," or "When is the first game of the NHL season?"

✔ Love stats? Find out information on players and teams by asking "Who has the most homeruns on the Texas Rangers?," "Who has the most goals in hockey?" or "Who has the highest slugging percentage in the MLB?" Or you can ask Siri "How often do the Yankees win on the road?" or "Who has the most points on the Vancouver Canucks?" You get the idea. See Figures 4-7 and 4-8 for examples.

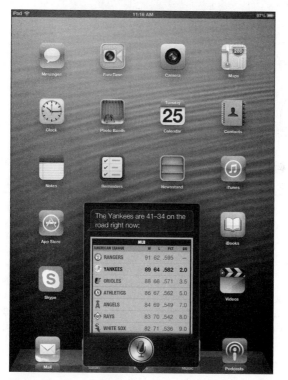

Figure 4-7: Siri is great for sports stats for both teams and individual players.

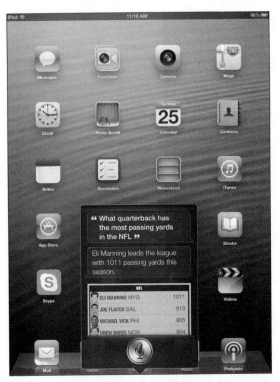

Figure 4-8: Ask about NFL passing and you'll even see headshots for the top players.

✔ Ask Siri about team rosters and you'll see the names of all the players as well as each player's jersey number, photo, position, and points. You also notice a quick summary of how the team is doing in the season (games won, lost, or tied) and the position in the league. See Figure 4-9. You can also ask Siri about injured players, such as "Is anyone on the Buffalo Bills injured?" (See Figure 4-10.) Or you can ask "Who is pitching today for Miami?" (see Figure 4-11).

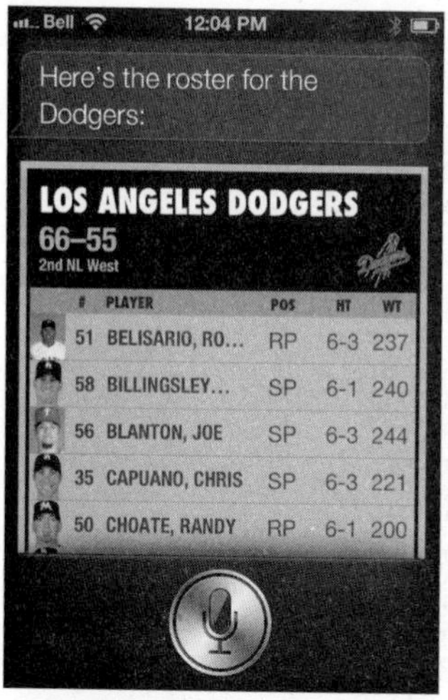

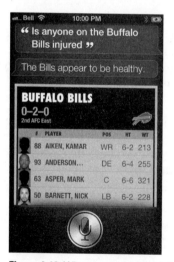

Figure 4-9: Siri can show you complete team rosters.

Figure 4-10: When you ask about injuries, Siri will give a quick summary and show you the current roster.

Figure 4-11: Find out who's pitching for your favorite baseball team just by asking.

Using Siri for Movie Info

If movies are your thing, Siri can help you get more out of feature films, thanks in part to a partnership with the experts at Rotten Tomatoes.

Whether you're after show times, reviews and ratings, runtime, or even a movie trailer, simply ask Siri about a film, cast, or crew and you'll get the info faster than you can say "Supercalifragilisticexpialidocious."

Got your popcorn? Lights, camera, action. . . .

Looking for movies near you

If you feel like a flick, look no further than Siri to see what's playing.

For example, you can find out where movie theaters are near you — or another address — by simply asking Siri.

Or, you can ask for a specific movie genre by movie studio or by saying the name of a film.

Here's what you can do, for example:

1. **Press and hold the Home button.**

   Hear the chime? That means Siri is listening.

2. **Ask Siri "What's playing near me?" or "What movies are playing?"**

   As shown in Figure 4-12, asking something so generic is likely to yield many results.

3. **Tap on the movie you're interested in.**

   Along with a synopsis of the movie, video trailer, Rotten Tomatoes reviews, and movie poster (see Figure 4-13), you can select a theater to see what time the film starts (see Figure 4-14).

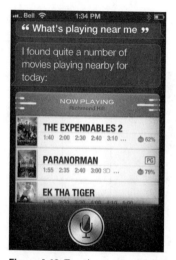

Figure 4-12: Tap the name of the film, such as *Paranorman,* for more info.

Figure 4-13: Watch a trailer, read the film synopsis, or tap the tomato for reviews at Rotten Tomatoes.

Figure 4-14: After you've selected the film, choose a theater and view its show times.

You can use other ways to see what's playing near you. Try these out with Siri when you get a chance:

✔ If you ask Siri to find movies, it will use the location of your iPhone, iPad, or iPod touch (Wi-Fi) to find nearby theaters automatically. But you can also search for movies based on another location. For example, you can ask Siri, "Find movie theaters in Decatur, Georgia (a suburb of Atlanta)." See Figure 4-15 for what shows up. Then you can tap the name of the theater you want to go to and you'll see a list of movies available there and the times they're playing. Alternatively, you can ask Siri something like "Find me movie theaters near my office" or "Locate movie theaters near my dad." If your father's address is in your Contacts, Siri will search for nearby theaters. Cool, huh?

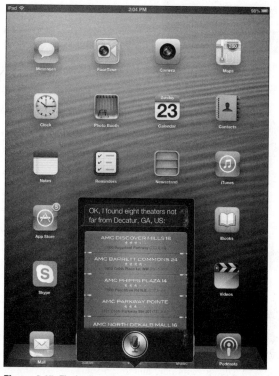

Figure 4-15: Find a list of theaters in a city, and then tap one for movie listings.

✔ Not sure what you feel like watching? Try asking Siri to find a movie by a star's name, genre, or movie studio (see Figures 4-16 and 4-17). Or try "What romantic comedies are playing?" Siri suggested Liberal Arts first and then showed older films.

Figure 4-16: Ask Siri to show you movie listings based on your favorite studio (such as Disney).

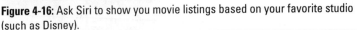

Figure 4-17: Tap a listing to see the full Rotten Tomatoes page for the film.

✔ You can ask Siri to find what's playing in other ways, too. Examples of what you can ask include "What's playing at Scotiabank Theater Toronto?" (a specific theater), "I want to see the new Paramount movie" (Siri might show you *Iron Man*, though hardly new), or "What's playing at the movies tomorrow?" In other words, the more information you give, the better Siri can provide you with what you want. You can also ask Siri something like "What's *The Expendables 2* rated?" and Siri will tell you the movie is rated R (Restricted). See Figure 4-18 as an example.

Figure 4-18: Are you about to take kids to a film? First ask Siri what the age rating is!

Asking Siri for movie info

Ever had tip-of-the-tongue syndrome? You know, where you can't remember a fact — such as the director of a particular film, who starred in this and that, or in what year did something come out? Well, instead of running to your computer to visit Internet Movie Database (IMDB), you can just ask Siri for this information and you'll get a fast and accurate response.

The following are a few examples of things you can ask Siri, when it comes to movie information:

✔ "Who starred in *The Shawshank Redemption*?" See Figure 4-19.

✔ "Who directed *The Big Lebowski*?"

✔ If you ask questions about costars, producers, or screenplay writers (for example, "Who costarred in *Jaws*?"), Siri shows you the Rotten Tomatoes page for the film.

✔ "What is the Rotten Tomatoes score for *The Lion King 1 ½*?" When I asked this, Siri said "Rotten Tomatoes gives *The Lion King 1 ½* a 73% rating," followed by multiple review quotes and summaries.

Figure 4-19: Don't pull your hair out when trying to figure out who starred in a movie. Just ask Siri.

Here's another way to ask for review information:

1. **Press and hold the Home button.**

   After the chime, you can ask away.

2. **Ask Siri "Show me the reviews for *The Dark Knight Rises*?" (See Figure 4-20.)**

   Of course, simply substitute the name of the movie for other flicks.

3. **Press the circle button on your device to exit out of Rotten Tomatoes.**

   Or just go about your business because there's no harm in leaving this page open.

Figure 4-20: Don't blow your hard-earned cash on a poorly reviewed movie. Scroll down to read all reviews.

Siri and Rotten Tomatoes can also present you with Academy Award information. For example, ask Siri "Which movie won Best Picture in 1995?" Siri replies with "*Forrest Gump,*" which won the Oscar for Best Picture in 1995. Wondering who won Best Supporting Actor in 1973? Siri says, "Here's *Cabaret* for which Joel Grey won the Oscar for Best Supporting Actor in 1973." See Figure 4-21.

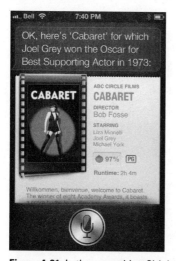

Figure 4-21: Is there anything Siri doesn't know? Within a second, this Rotten Tomatoes info was displayed when asked.

Don't bother asking Siri for Golden Globe awards because you won't likely get an accurate response. For example, I asked "What won Best Picture, Drama, at the 2005 Golden Globes?" and instead, Siri showed me every movie since 1950 that was nominated for Best Picture at the Golden Globes. (The answer, by the way, is *The Aviator.*)

Asking Siri for movie trailers

There are thousands of Apple movie trailers at Rotten Tomatoes, so all you need to do is ask Siri to play one based on a movie you want to see, and it'll start right away.

Not all movies are supported, as I was told there wasn't a trailer for *Finding Nemo* (but found it online instead), but more often than not Siri will find one — especially for newer films. And yes, you can also find trailers to films that aren't in theaters yet.

Here's how to ask for a trailer:

1. **Press and hold the Home button.**

   After the chime, speak loud and clear.

2. **Ask Siri to show you a movie trailer, such as "Show me a trailer for *The Hunger Games*." (See Figure 4-22.)**

   Give it a second, and Siri will verbally confirm your request.

Figure 4-22: Just before the trailer, you'll see a summary of the film you asked about.

3. **Watch the trailer on your iPhone, iPad, or iPod touch. (See Figure 4-23.) Then, press the circle button to exit.**

   You can also tap to play the trailer again or pause it if you need to stop it momentarily.

Figure 4-23: The Apple trailer for the film will begin to play on the iGadget, and you don't need to touch a thing.

Asking Siri about Restaurants

Siri can also help you discover new restaurants, provide directions, and even book reservations. Now Siri offers a lot more than just listing restaurants in a given location. Your voice-activated personal assistant can sort by price, cuisine, stars, and reviews from Yelp (a popular site for business listings and ratings), or other variables of your choosing, such as a restaurant that offers a patio for outdoor seating. Siri can now show you photos of a restaurant, too.

Having Siri find you a restaurant

Siri is great for sifting through information to provide you with what you want — and restaurants are no exception. Feel like a burger? Greek food? Indian cuisine? Vegan fare? Simply ask Siri. (Yes, that's the mantra of this book — simply ask Siri!)

The first way to search is by location and cuisine, so you can ask Siri to find something "near me" — and because your iPhone or iPad is location-aware, Siri knows where you are, geographically speaking. Even if you don't add "near me" when you ask Siri something like "Find me a good Mexican restaurant," by default, Siri will *think* you want something nearby.

Canadians, by the way, will be happy to know that their country is now officially supported when it comes to restaurant search (and other businesses) as well as turn-by-turn directions.

You can also ask for a restaurant in another city altogether, perhaps to recommend something to a family member or to book a reservation before leaving on an important business trip or vacation.

Here's how to ask for a restaurant by cuisine or location:

1. **Press and hold the Home button.**

   Speak to Siri after the short chime.

2. **Ask Siri to list restaurants by cuisine (for example, vegetarian, Thai, or pizza) and, if you like, by location.**

   For example, ask "Find a Thai restaurant near me" or "Find a good burger restaurant in Spokane" (near me or in Chicago, for example).

   Siri will quickly search and show you relevant results. See Figures 4-24 and 4-25 as examples.

3. **Now you can tap one of the selections for contact information, photos, reviews, and directions.**

   You can also tap in the top-left corner to go back.

You probably noticed the little dollar signs next to each restaurant listing. Yelp is showing you how much the meal should cost, relatively speaking, compared with other restaurants. One dollar sign is inexpensive, two dollar signs suggest the cost is about average, three dollar signs is somewhat pricey, and four dollar signs means you can expect to pay more than other restaurants.

Tapping on one of the restaurant listings provided by Siri, pulls up that particular establishment's Details page on Yelp. This page includes

- ✔ The cuisine type (Asian Fusion, for example).
- ✔ How much money you can expect to pay there.
- ✔ The hours of operation as well as whether the restaurant is open or closed, based on what time you're looking at this page.

✓ The average Yelp score out of 5 stars. Tap the score for individual reviews from past patrons.

✓ A couple of photos of the restaurant (if available).

✓ Contact information, including phone number, address, website, how far the place is from you, and a map showing where it is near you. Tap the map to launch the Maps app, including turn-by-turn directions.

✓ If you have the Yelp app installed, tap the Yelp logo to take you to the restaurant's official page within the app, for even more information.

Figure 4-24: Craving good Mexican food? (Doesn't everyone?) Here's what Siri recommends near me.

Figure 4-25: You can ask for cuisine and location together, such as in another city.

See Figures 4-26, 4-27, and 4-28 for examples of a typical restaurant's Yelp page on an iPhone.

Figure 4-26: A Yelp restaurant page, after tapping on one of Siri's recommendations.

Figure 4-27: Tap the small map (near the bottom) to launch the Maps app for a bigger view, directions, and more.

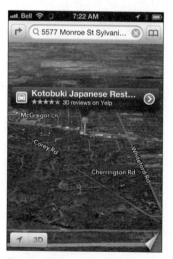

Figure 4-28: Here's a look at this Japanese restaurant on the Maps app.

You can also ask Siri for top-rated restaurants — regardless of the cuisine — and through Yelp, Siri will pull up all the highest rated options in the city you asked for. For example, I asked for the highest rated restaurants in San Francisco and the first few displayed were all 4.5 stars out of 5 and with more than 2,000 reviews per establishment.

Want to see the restaurant's menu? Although Siri can't help there (er, yet), you can still see what's cooking at a particular place. When you're on the restaurant's Yelp page, tap the website to open up the official site in Safari. Now you can peruse the restaurant's menu (and prices) before you get there.

You can also grab your iPhone, iPad, or iPod touch and ask for reviews of specific restaurants without narrowing it down by cuisine or location. For example, you can say, "Show me the reviews for Lavo in Las Vegas," and you'll see the Yelp score and reviews right away.

Using Siri to book a reservation for you

Siri can now book your restaurant reservations, courtesy of OpenTable.

That's right, it's one thing to read reviews of restaurants, view photos, and see where it's located in the city, but you can also book a table in a matter of seconds (really).

You can ask for a reservation at a particular restaurant (and time), a kind of cuisine, a city, or leave it with Siri to recommend something by simply asking "Book a reservation for two tomorrow night."

You need to have the OpenTable app installed on your iOS device. It's free, but it requires registration, including some information about you (such as a phone number in case the restaurant needs to contact you).

Here's how to do it:

1. **Press and hold the Home button.**

   After the beep, speak to Siri.

2. **Ask Siri something like "Make a reservation for two at an Italian restaurant tonight."**

   Siri shows you a list of restaurants that meet your criteria, if they have tables available — and at what time, as shown in Figure 4-29.

3. **Now you can tap one of the selections and review details, such as time (or change it), address, price, or read reviews. See Figure 4-30.**

Also, the website address is here, to peruse the menu and prices.

Figure 4-29: Mamma mia! These Italian restaurants have tables available tonight.

Figure 4-30: Access the Details page within Yelp.

4. **Tap Make Reservation to open the OpenTable app on your iPhone, iPad, or iPod touch. See Figure 4-31.** (I erased my e-mail address and phone number here.)

This takes you out of Siri, but you'll get the reservation you want on the spot.

Figure 4-31: Review the details in the OpenTable app and tap to confirm. Bon appetit!

Chapter 5

Using Siri for E-Mail, Texting, and Phone Calls

. . . .

In This Chapter

▶ Sending an e-mail using your voice — even to multiple people at once

▶ Using the CC and BCC fields

▶ Having Siri find e-mails in your inbox

▶ Replying and forwarding e-mail messages

▶ Composing text messages through Siri

▶ Having Siri read your text messages to you

▶ Using your voice to make phone calls and initiate FaceTime calls

. . . .

In this chapter — and it's one of the longer ones — you get to see how you can use Siri as your personal communication tool.

Specifically, your voice-activated personal assistant on iPhone, iPad, or iPod touch can be very handy for composing and accessing e-mails, composing and reading iMessages and text messages (SMS), and for iPhone users, placing a phone call to a particular number or someone in your Contacts (address book).

There's quite a lot to cover, so I want to jump right in and begin.

"Siri, Take a Letter"

One of the most impressive — and convenient — things Siri can do is send your e-mails for you.

Siri can transcribe your words into text so that you only need to talk into your iPhone, iPad, or iPod touch. Siri will then type out the words you say, including the name of the person or group you're sending it to, the subject line, and the body of the message.

You'll find this can really speed up your "written" communication on your favorite iDevice. In fact, experts say talking is three to four times faster than typing. Plus, not everyone is as fast or accurate on an all-touch smartphone as they are on those button-based ones out there. (Think BlackBerry smartphones.)

In other words, using Siri for sending e-mails not only catches up to other phones, but blows past it.

In this chapter, I show you how to use Siri to send e-mails to family, friends, and colleagues — whether they're in your Contacts or not.

Although using Siri to type e-mails for you is incredibly convenient, resist doing it while you're behind the wheel of a moving vehicle. You still may need to glance at your phone to catch small errors — or at the very least you might be preoccupied with your e-mail instead of concentrating on driving — so be sure to send your messages after you've parked the car. After all, Siri can't call 9-1-1 for you.

Composing, Sending, and Accessing E-Mails

You have two ways to start composing an e-mail using Siri. You can start right from your home screen — as if you just turned on your smartphone, tablet, or media player — by pressing and holding the Home button (or if it's set up to do so, by holding your iPhone up to your ear). The other way to have Siri transcribe your words into text is to start a message to someone the old-fashioned way (typing), and then tap the microphone icon to start talking. Figure 5-1 shows you what you might see if you were to talk into your iOS device.

Here's a closer look at both options.

Figure 5-1: Siri types your spoken e-mails for you.

Starting and sending an e-mail from scratch

Okay, so you realize you need to send an e-mail to someone while you're walking down the street and you don't want to stop to type the message. There is a better way. Pull out your smartphone, press the Home button, and then start talking.

In this section, I explain the *simplest* way to send an e-mail. I cover the *fastest* way to send an e-mail later in the chapter.

Here's the blow-by-blow account for starting an e-mail using Siri:

1. **Press and hold the Home button.**

   The little chime you hear means Siri is listening for your instructions.

2. **Say the word "E-mail" and then the name of the person you want to e-mail.**

   Siri opens your mail program and puts the name of the person you're e-mailing in the To field — if they're in your address book. (See the "E-mailing someone who isn't in your Contacts" section, later in this chapter, to find out how to e-mail someone who isn't in your Contacts.)

3. **Dictate your e-mail.**

   When you're done, Siri shows you the contents of your message on the screen, as shown in Figure 5-2. For example, you can say "E-mail Mary Smith [short pause]. Hi Mary, hope you're having a good day. This is just a reminder about our meeting at 3 p.m. See you then."

   Take advantage of the fact that Siri previews your e-mail by showing you the contents of your message on the screen by taking the time to review your e-mail, just in case you need to tweak it, add more recipients, and so on, before sending it.

   Siri next asks you, "What's the subject of your e-mail?"

Figure 5-2: Siri lets you review your e-mail before sending it.

4. **Say what you'd like the subject line to say, such as, "Meeting confirmation."**

   Siri again shows you what your e-mail currently looks like — now you should be able to see the person you're sending it to, what the subject is, and the body of the e-mail. Siri says, "Here's what your e-mail looks like. Ready to send it?" If you're in fact ready to send it, you can let 'er fly.

5. **Review all fields, and then say, "Okay," "Yes," "No," or "Cancel."**

   Alternatively, you can tap the appropriate response — Cancel or Send— if you prefer.

   If you say "Yes" or tap Send, then it's bye-bye e-mail. Your e-mail message is sent, and you'll hear that "whoosh" sound as a confirmation.

   If you say "No" or tap Cancel, the message is canceled, and you'll see a large red CANCELED stamp across the message. It won't be saved as a draft.

It might take you a bit to get the hang of composing and sending e-mails with Siri. When you're starting an e-mail, remember that you can do these things:

✔ **Teach Siri who your contacts are.** When you're starting an e-mail and say, "E-mail Dad," for the first time, Siri asks who your dad is. You're prompted to tap the contact name in your Contacts listing for your dad.

   You can edit your own Contacts entry (your name) and scroll down to see where you can add relationships, such as spouse, parents, and so forth.

   Going forward, you can simply say, "E-mail Dad," and Siri knows whose address to retrieve; you won't have to tap the name again.

✔ **Correct mistakes and make other changes.** If you make a mistake and need to change your e-mail, say, "Change subject," or "Change e-mail," and then give Siri a revised message for the recipient. In Figure 5-3, for example, Siri misspelled my name (Mark instead of Marc, believe it or not), but it allowed me to correct the mistake by repeating the request a few times and Siri, the third time, finally showed me "Marc" instead of "Mark," and so I accepted. This *usually* works.

Figure 5-3: Siri allows you to edit messages.

✔ **Tell Siri which e-mail address to send a message to.** If you have multiple e-mail addresses for someone in your Contacts, you can instruct Siri to e-mail a specific address. For example, you might have a friend with a work and home e-mail address, and don't want to send a private message about an upcoming party to your best friend's work address. Simply tell Siri "E-mail [friend's name]," followed by "[work or home]," followed by "[message]." Also, if you have more than one, say, Mary Smith in your Contacts, it might ask you to select one over another.

✔ **Cancel messages.** To cancel the message altogether, say "No" or "Cancel" when Siri asks you if it's OK to send the message.

You can always tap the microphone button to cancel your last request.

If you want to make sure that Siri understood you, check to see if a large red CANCELED stamp appears across your e-mail message, as shown in Figure 5-4.

✔ **Have Siri type the subject line first.** To do so, say "subject" right after you say the receiver's name, and Siri regards the next few words out of your mouth as the subject line, as shown in Figure 5-5. Only after she enters the subject does she prompt you to dictate the body of the e-mail.

For example, say "E-Mail Mary Smith [slight pause], work, subject [slight pause], meeting confirmation." Now, press the Home button or wait a second, and Siri will ask you, "Okay, what would you like the e-mail to say?" Now you can dictate the body of the e-mail and have Siri send it for you, hands-free.

Figure 5-4: A large CANCELED stamp appears across any message you choose not to send.

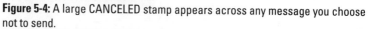

Figure 5-5: Say the e-mail subject line first and then dictate the body.

Having Siri finish an e-mail you started to type

The second way you can send an e-mail using your voice is to start an e-mail the regular way — by tapping the E-mail icon and then tapping to select to whom you're sending the message. The screen shown in Figure 5-6 appears. Notice the microphone icon at the bottom of the screen, to the left of the spacebar. Simply tap that icon and begin dictating into the iPhone, iPad, or iPod touch; you'll see your words appear on the white canvas, as if you were typing them yourself. Before you send it, however, quickly scan for errors.

Figure 5-6: Tap the microphone icon to dictate your e-mail inside the message.

 Did you know you can also fold the subject into your e-mail message at the same time you ask Siri to start it for you? For example, you can say, "E-mail my wife about the vacation," and Siri will start a message for you to your wife (because you've already told Siri who she is) and the word "vacation" will be in the subject line because it follows the word "about." Next, Siri will ask you, "What do you want the e-mail to say?"

 If you're really ambitious, you can have Siri create an e-mail for you, populate the To field, give a subject, and type the message for you — all in one breath. In other words, you can tell Siri where to send the e-mail, the subject line, and the body of the e-mail all at once, therefore it's a much faster way to do it. Not many folks know this trick, but it's one of my favorite Siri demos to perform for people! As you can see in Figure 5-7, I gave Siri all of this info at the same time: "E-mail Mike Jones about the article and say Hi Mike, I think this should work." Talk about a time saver, huh? Another example is "E-mail Mom and Dad about the luncheon and say I had a great time," and Siri will populate all the fields of the e-mail message for you. Try it — you'll like it!

Figure 5-7: Siri lets you say all three parts to the e-mail, all in one shot.

Sending e-mail to groups

You can have Siri send an e-mail to a number of people at once — and you won't believe how easy it is. Just follow these steps:

1. **Say everyone's name you want to e-mail the message to.**

   For instance, say, "Send an e-mail to Dad and my wife and Mary Smith and Mike Jones."

   You must say "and" in between each of the recipients' names. If Siri is unsure about someone (such as having three contacts with the name Kellie or Kelly), Siri will ask you to confirm which one you want to send the correspondence to.

   Siri asks, "What would you like to say to these four people?" and you'll see them all in the To field, as shown in Figure 5-8.

2. **Answer Siri by dictating your group message.**

   Siri asks if you're ready to send it.

3. **Say "Yes" to send the message.**

   You'll hear the familiar confirmation sound, confirming that the message was sent.

Figure 5-8: A message to a group looks like a message to a single recipient.

4. **(Optional) If you need to tweak a couple of things, tap anywhere on the screen and make your changes before sending.**

   If you decide to manually tweak your message, the e-mail now looks like one you may have typed from the get-go. (See Figure 5-9.)

Siri e-mail grab bag

Siri is multitalented, so you might have trouble keeping up with all she can do. The following list gives you an idea of the range of things Siri can do:

✔ **Send an e-mail while wearing a headset, microphone, or Bluetooth headset.** If you're using headphones with a remote and microphone on the cord, simply press and hold the center button to talk to Siri. If you're wearing a Bluetooth headset, on the other hand, press and hold the call button to bring up Siri's tone, which means you can begin asking a question or giving a command. Keep in mind, however, that speakerphones in your vehicle might not work as well with Siri, because your mouth is farther away from the microphone, which can pick up more background noise.

✔ **If you're unsure what Siri can do, just ask!** You can literally ask your personal assistant what she (a female voice in North America) is capable of, and you'll see a laundry list of things she can perform for you. If you want specific examples, tap one of Siri's initial suggestions. For instance, if you want to know how to use Siri for sending e-mails, tap the line that says "E-mail Lisa about the trip," and this will open up a dozen more examples of ways to use Siri for e-mail.

✔ **Include punctuation in an e-mail message.** To do so, just say it out loud. For example, to finish a sentence you can say, "period." Asking a question? Be sure to say, "question mark," at the end of the sentence. You can also say, "exclamation mark," "comma," "semicolon," "quote" (or "quotation mark"), and so on.

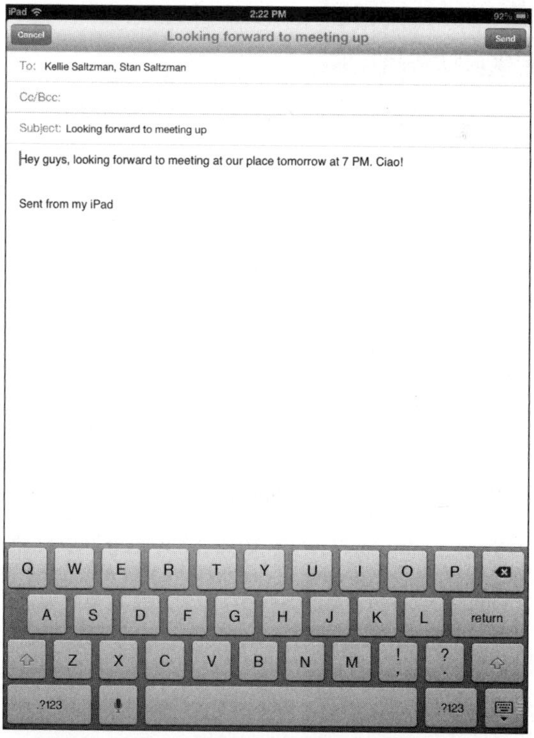

Figure 5-9: Tap anywhere on the screen to make changes.

You can even say, "smiley face," and you'll see the emoticon (sideways smiley face) on the screen! See Figure 5-10 for an example of Siri's work — with 100 percent accuracy, no less. Also try saying "frowny face" (when you're not happy) or "winky face" (sly, flirty).

Figure 5-10: Testing the punctuation options, including "exclamation mark" and "smiley face."

Table 5-1, 5-2, and 5-3 list many *formatting, punctuation, financial,* and *mathematical* commands to create the perfect e-mail using Siri on your iPhone, iPad, or new iPod touch. Most of these commands will work in a text message or the Notes app, too. On the left is what you should say to perform the design action on the right.

Table 5-1	Formatting Commands
When You Say This	*Siri Does This*
"new line"	Moves down to the next line (as though you've pressed Return or Enter on a computer keyboard)
"new paragraph"	Starts a new paragraph
"caps on"	Capitalizes all following words
"caps off"	Turns off capitalization

Table 5-2	Punctuation Commands
When You Say This	*Siri Adds This*
"period" or "dot"	.
"ellipsis" or "dot dot dot"	...
"dash" or "hyphen"	–
"em dash"	— (double-length dash)
"comma"	,
"underscore"	_
"forward slash"	/
"back slash"	\
"vertical bar"	|
"quote" or "quotation mark"	" (until you say "quote" or "quotation mark" again)
"exclamation point"	!
"question mark"	?
"ampersand"	&
"asterisk"	*
"at sign"	@
"copyright sign"	©
"registered sign"	®
"degree sign"	°
"caret"	^
"open parenthesis" or "close parenthesis"	(or)
"open bracket" or "close bracket"	[or]
"open brace" or "close brace"	{ or }

Table 5-3	Math and Finance Commands
When You Say This	**Siri Adds This**
"plus sign"	+
"minus sign"	-
"equals sign"	=
"percent sign"	%
"dollar sign"	$
"cent sign"	¢
"pound sterling" sign	£
"pound sign"	#
"euro sign"	€
"yen sign"	¥
"degree sign"	°
"caret"	^
"greater than sign"	>
"less than sign"	<

CCing and BCCing contacts in an e-mail

Just like in a regular e-mail, you can send an e-mail to one person and carbon copy, or CC, another person, so they also receive the same e-mail as the main recipient.

As you'd expect with Siri, all you need to do is send an e-mail to someone (in my example from Figure 5-11, that person is Mary Smith) and then take a short pause, say "CC," then mention someone else from your Contacts (in this case, Mike Jones). Then you can say "subject" and tell Siri what you want your subject line to be.

Alternatively, you can say "carbon copy" instead of "CC." Figure 5-12 shows this method works, too.

Figure 5-11: Saying "CC" keeps someone else in the loop.

Figure 5-12: Saying "carbon copy" works too.

And of course, you can also "BCC" or *blind carbon copy* someone when sending an e-mail. For the uninitiated, specifying "BCC" means someone else *is* included on the e-mail — but the main recipient (and perhaps people you've also CC'd) won't have a clue because they won't see any mention of the other person's name or e-mail address.

It's considered proper *netiquette* (Internet etiquette) not to blitz a number of people at once and reveal all of their e-mail addresses to everyone. To respect people's privacy, it's better to BCC people instead. Doing it with Siri is simple: Just say, "BCC," or "blind carbon copy," and say the person(s) e-mail address you want to hide and you'll see that person's name appear in the BCC area of your e-mail message. For an example of this technique, check out Figure 5-13.

Of course, you can CC one person (or many people) and BCC someone else (or a whole bunch of somebody else's) within the same e-mail.

Figure 5-13: Add e-mail recipients to the blind carbon copy field of the message by simply saying "BCC."

More E-Mail Tasks Siri Can Do for You

As late-night infomercial guru Ron Popeil says, "But wait; there's more!" Siri can also do these e-mail–related tasks for you.

E-mailing someone who isn't in your Contacts

In earlier sections of this chapter, I discuss e-mailing people who are already in your Contacts. But what if you need to send an e-mail to someone who's not listed there?

Using Siri to send an e-mail to a specific address — one you might not have in your Contacts or care to add — is as simple as speaking the address aloud.

Here's how to do it:

1. **Press and hold the Home button and tell Siri to send an e-mail to someone by saying their complete e-mail address.**

   For example, to send an e-mail to `richard.anderson@ bigtimeisp.com` (just making this one up), simply say, "E-mail Richard dot Anderson at bigtimeisp dot com."

   The e-mail address appears in the To field, as shown in Figure 5-14.

2. **Add a subject and dictate your e-mail.**

   Siri transcribes your words, and then asks if you're ready to send the e-mail.

Figure 5-14: Asking Siri to enter an e-mail address.

3. **(Optional) If you need to tweak a couple of things, tap anywhere on the screen and make your changes before sending.**

4. **Say, "Yes," to send the message.**

   The iPhone, iPad, and iPod touch confirmation sound confirms the message was sent.

   Siri won't add this person to your Contacts.

Finding e-mails in your inbox

Guess what? Siri isn't only good for transcribing your voice into e-mail messages. Siri can also help you find e-mails:

✔ **Most recent messages:** For example, say you have a few hundred messages in your inbox but you want to find the most recent ones? You can simply tell Siri, "Check e-mail" and you'll immediately see the last 25 e-mail messages that arrived in your inbox.

✔ **From a specific person:** You can ask, "Any new e-mail from Matt today?" and Siri will show you any e-mails received today from anyone named Matt. Or you can say, "Show the e-mail from Lisa yesterday." Figure 5-15 shows the kinds of things such a request might pull up.

✔ **Based on the subject line:** You can tell Siri, "Show new e-mail about the doctor's appointment," or "Show e-mail about the rent," and Siri will pull up any relevant messages for you.

Figure 5-15: The result of asking Siri whether I've received an e-mail from "Matt."

Replying to and forwarding messages

Siri won't just send an e-mail for you. It's also possible to reply to or forward an e-mail you've already received. For example, while you're reading an e-mail you can hold down the Home button and tell Siri, "Reply Dear Julie, sorry I had to cancel plans for Saturday's lunch. I'll call you later to chat about another date."

To forward a message, press and hold the Home button while inside of the e-mail and say something like, "Forward e-mail to Phil." Siri will ask you if you want to add a message as well ("What do you want the e-mail to say?"). See Figure 5-16 for an example of me forwarding a note to my wife, Kellie.

Figure 5-16: In this example, I told Siri to forward this e-mail message to my wife, Kellie.

Composing, Replying to, and Reading Text Messages

Siri is great when it comes to composing, sending, forwarding, and accessing all your e-mails on your iPhone, iPad, or iPod touch, but don't for a second think that Siri can deal with only e-mail. If you're of an age to think e-mail is old school and that texting is the wave of the future, that won't throw Siri for a loop. She can text with the best of them.

You might already be using the Messages app bundled on your smartphone, tablet, or iPod touch — who can resist such a quick, reliable, and inexpensive way to communicate with friends and family between phones (regardless of the model?) — but Siri makes it even more handy. And frankly, texting is now a lot more fun, too.

Not only can you use Siri to dictate text messages for you, just as you do for e-mail, but Siri can also read your unread text messages aloud, too! (Nope, Siri can't do this for e-mails but she can for texts.) Now you can continue your jog down the beach without pulling out your smartphone and you can ask Siri to read your texts out loud to you. How convenient, eh?

This portion of the chapter outlines how texting with Siri works, including what you need to say for it to work smoothly, and what you'll hear back as a response.

Composing a text message

Sending a text message with your voice is incredibly fast and accurate.

There are a couple of different ways to text using Siri. If you'd like to do it one step at a time, the following is the most basic way to compose a text message:

1. **Press and hold the Home button.**

   Wait for the short chime and begin speaking.

2. **Say the word "Text" and then the name of the person you want to send a text message to.**

   Siri opens your iMessage app and puts the name of the person you're texting in the To field — if he or she is in your Contacts, that is. Flip forward a few pages to see how to text someone who isn't in your Contacts.

3. **In response to Siri's prompt ("What do you want your message to say?"), dictate your text message.**

   When you're done, Siri shows you the message and asks you if you want to send it.

4. Say "Yes" or "Send" to send the message. Or say "No" or "Cancel" to cancel the message.

If it's sent, you'll hear the standard whoosh confirmation sound, and the message disappears. (To see it, open up your iMessage app and see the conversation tree with that particular person; your sent texts will be in green.) Figure 5-17 shows what a typical text message would look like, as transcribed by Siri.

If you choose not to send a text message you've composed, Siri will ask you what you'd like to do with the message, as shown in Figure 5-18. At the top of the screen, you'll see, "To continue, you can Send, Cancel, Review, or Change it." As you'd expect, saying "Send" sends the text; "Cancel" cancels the message; "Review" reads it to you; and "Change" lets you tweak using the keyboard, if need be.

You don't always have to say the word "Text" to tell Siri you want to start a text message. You can also say something like, "Message," or "Tell," followed by the person or phone number you want to send the text message to! Try it and use what's most comfortable for you.

。Il Bell 令   11:48 AM   ▌ ⊡

❝ Text Susan McKenzie hi Susan, are we still on for lunch? ❞

Here's your message to Susan McKenzie.

To: Susan McKenzie

Hi Susan, are we still on for lunch?

Cancel   Send

Figure 5-17: Texting is as easy as saying, "Text," followed by the name of the person you want to send the message to.

Figure 5-18: You're given options if you tell Siri not to send the message.

Another way to compose a text message is to say the person's name you want to text and the message — all in one breath, without waiting for Siri's prompt. Because texts are usually shorter than e-mails, you might opt to do this to save time. Don't worry; Siri can handle this without a hitch.

An example of what this might look like follows:

1. **Press and hold the Home button.**

   Begin talking after the chime.

2. **Tell Siri, "Text" and the person's name; after a very short pause, say the message aloud, too.**

   You'll hear a high ping, which means Siri is processing your command, and then you'll see your text message.

3. **Review the text message and, if it looks good to you, say "Send" or "Yes." (If it doesn't look good, say "No" or "Cancel" to cancel the message.)**

   Siri will do what you ask, of course. That's her job as your faithful personal assistant. Figure 5-19 shows an example of a canceled message.

Figure 5-19: Just like a canceled e-mail, Siri stamps the word CANCELED in red.

If you have a few different phone numbers for someone in your address book, you might find it easier to specify what number to send the text message to right away. For example, tell Siri, "Message Susan on her mobile that I'll be late for our 2 p.m. coffee." Saying "on her mobile" eliminates any doubt Siri might have about what number to send the text to.

Texting more than one person

Just as you can send an e-mail to multiple people through Siri, it's also possible to compose and send an iMessage or traditional text message to more than one recipient. (For sending group e-mails, see earlier in this chapter on how to pull that off via Siri.)

In fact, this can really help save you time. All you need to do is ask Siri to send the text to multiple people, like this:

1. **Press and hold the Home button.**

   When you hear a short chime, you know that Siri is ready for you.

2. **Tell Siri "Text" the name of the first person you'd like to text, "and," and the name of the second person.**

   It's important you say the word "and" between all the names!

You can add as many people as you like. You can also wait for Siri to respond with, "What would you like the message to say?" or start saying the message after you tell Siri to whom you're sending the message (a short pause is best). Figure 5-20 shows what a request for a text message to multiple recipients looks like. You don't need to say or touch anything to go to the text view shown in Figure 5-21.

3. **Review the text message (refer to Figure 5-21) and, if you like what you see, say "Yes" or "Send." If not, say "No" or "Cancel" and you'll be prompted with other options, as shown earlier, in Figure 5-18.**

   If you opt for "Yes" or "Send," Siri sends the same text message to multiple recipients.

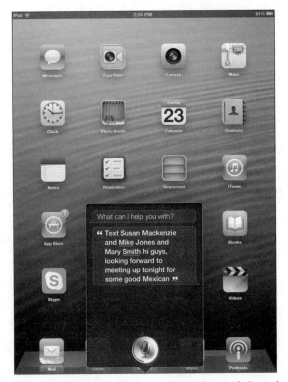

Figure 5-20: Siri transcribes your instructions and shows it to you before opening the iMessage app.

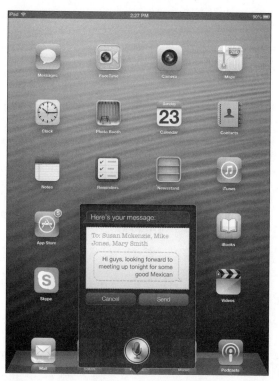

Figure 5-21: The text message to multiple people looks like this.

As you can see in Figure 5-21, you sometimes won't be able to see all the recipients Siri will send the text message to. If this concerns you — for fear of sending the text to the wrong person — you can tap the screen, which opens up the text message within iMessage, and you'll see all additional recipients listed clearly here.

If punctuation is important to you, remember to say things like "comma," "period," and "question mark" inside your text message.

Composing a text message from within Messages

Just like e-mailing on your iOS device, you can start a text message the old-fashioned way — by opening up Messages and selecting to whom the note will be sent — but then finish it off with your voice, if you like.

Perhaps you decide it would be faster to dictate your text message instead of typing it out. You don't need to close down the message and start again.

Here's what you do:

1. **In Messages, tap the icon of a little microphone, just to the left of the space bar. (See Figure 5-22.)**

2. **Speak your text message clearly, then tap the word Done when you're finished.**

   Siri shows your words on the screen.

3. **If what you see onscreen is accurate — the words are what you said — then tap the green Send button to the right of the speech window.**

   Siri sends your text message.

Figure 5-22: See that little microphone icon? Tap it to begin speaking.

If you're e-mailing or Messaging with someone and want to send a phone number, don't waste your breath by saying "dash" between the numbers of a 10-digit phone number. Siri knows you're giving a phone number if you have the word "call," "number" or "phone" in the body of the message, too. You knew Siri was smart, so why are you so surprised? For example, as you can see in Figure 5-23, I gave my (fictitious) phone number to someone inside an iMessage and I didn't say "dash" or "hyphen" after the area code and between the third and fourth numbers. I simply said "2121231234" and Siri cleverly wrote it out for me as 212-123-1234.

Figure 5-23: You need not say "dash" when giving out your phone number. Siri should know when (and where) to place the dashes in a 10-digit number.

Hearing Your Text Messages Read Aloud

Ah, this is one of the coolest features of Siri: the option to hear your texts read out loud to you.

Say you've got a bunch of unread text messages and iMessages on your iPhone, iPad, or iPod touch and you don't want to tap through each one. After all, you might be concentrating on something you're looking at — er, like the road in front of your vehicle.

Siri can read your text messages to you in a human-like voice, and you can even respond to them using your voice, too. Now that's hands-free.

Here's how to have Siri read your text messages out loud:

1. **Press and hold the Home button.**

   After the short chime, you can give Siri a command.

2. **Say something like, "Read me my texts." See Figure 5-24.**

   You can make the same request a number of different ways. "Do I have any messages?" works just great.

   Siri announces how many messages you have waiting for you. Siri then starts reading all new messages to you, beginning with the sender's name — or if the name is unknown, the phone number it's coming from. You won't see the message on the screen.

3. **When prompted by Siri to say what you want to do with the message, say either "Reply" or "Read them again."**

   Siri performs the action requested. See Figure 5-25 for an example of my reply to my wife Kellie's text message.

 Keep in mind that Siri will read only those text messages that you haven't picked up yet. If you've got a bunch of messages stored on your device but you've already read and/or replied to them, Siri will tell you there isn't anything to read to you. Figure 5-26 shows you what you'd hear and see on your iPhone screen in such a situation.

Figure 5-24: Though you don't see the words here, Siri is reading my new texts to me aloud.

Figure 5-25: Say "Reply" and dictate your reply to the sender. Siri sends the message when you're done.

Figure 5-26: Siri tells me there are no new messages because she speaks the text of only unread messages.

You have a number of options when it comes to responding to a text message. The following are a few commands that Siri can handle:

 ✔ **"Reply that's a great idea, thanks."**

 ✔ **"Reply saying that's a great idea, thanks."**

✔ "Tell her I'll be there in 15 minutes."

✔ "Call him."

✔ "E-mail her."

✔ "Read it again."

Sending a Text Message to a Phone Number

Okay, so say you're given a phone number to text, but it isn't stored in your Contacts. No problem, as Siri can be used to send a text to a 10-digit number, if you prefer.

Maybe you don't want to add someone to your address book or it's a one-time text (such as a contest you need to enter via SMS).

All you need to do is say the phone number you want to text, and Siri will know what to do. For instance, do this:

1. **Press and hold the Home button.**

   Siri chimes, letting you know you can start talking.

2. **Tell Siri the phone number to text.**

   As an example, tell Siri, "Text 212-555-1212 [short pause]. Enter me in the drawing, thanks."

   You can also say, "Message," or "Tell," instead of "Text."

   Siri shows you the number you want to send the text message to as well as your message.

3. **After previewing the number and text message, say "Yes" or "Send," and Siri will do the rest. If you don't want to send the text, say "No" or "Cancel."**

   See Figure 5-27 for an example of texting a number instead of the name of someone in your Contacts.

Siri won't decipher acronyms or text-speak, so if someone sends you a message with "LOL" or "TTYL," Siri won't say "laugh out loud" or "talk to you later," respectively.

Also be aware that you can't send a picture or video message via Siri. If you said, "Text a photo to my wife," it won't ask you which photo to attach; instead Siri will think you want to text the words "a photo" to your wife.

Figure 5-27: Sending a text to a phone number is as easy as saying a name.

Calling a Number or Person (and Starting FaceTime Chats, Too!)

The final part of this chapter covers how you can use Siri to call someone in your Contacts or any phone number you want to call.

Okay, calling a phone number isn't the most ground-breaking thing Siri can do — cellphones have been able to "voice dial" for many years now — but you'll find Siri is a lot more accurate at the task. How many times have you said into an old phone "Call home" and your phone replies with "Calling Dr. Lome." Sigh.

As with all other Siri tasks, all you have to do is ask Siri to perform a task, and she will comply:

1. **Press and hold the Home button.**

2. **Wait for the short chime and then give Siri the command.**

For example, you can say "Call" and give the person's name.

As long as the person is in your Contacts, Siri will call the person for you.

If you have multiple phone numbers for an individual, Siri might not know which phone number to use. That's why she may (politely) ask for a bit of clarification, as shown in Figure 5-28.

Figure 5-28: Tell Siri the person you want to call. Siri might ask to confirm which number to dial (work, home, and so on).

If you know that a contact listing has multiple phone numbers, you can specify which number to dial, like this:

1. **Press and hold the Home button.**

2. **Begin talking after the short chime.**

   You could say "Call [person's name] mobile." Or "Call [person's name] home." Or "Call [person's name] work."

   You get the idea. Siri knows which number to call because you're more specific. (See Figures 5-29 and 5-30.)

You can tell Siri who the important people are in your life — such as "husband," "mom," or "brother" — and Siri remembers. For instance, after you tell Siri your wife's name and Siri associates "wife" with the appropriate Contacts listing, you can tell Siri to "Call my wife on her work phone," and the task will be performed. You can also specify your home and office numbers for Siri; after doing that, you can say things like, "Call home."

Figure 5-29: Specify which telephone number Siri should dial.

Figure 5-30: Siri dials the number you requested, such as "home," "office," or "mobile."

If you want to call a phone number that's not in your Contacts, you can do it by saying the 10-digit number verbally:

1. **Press and hold the Home button.**

2. **Tell Siri what you'd like — but wait for the familiar chime first.**

You can say "Call" and give the phone number. Or say "Dial" and give the phone number. (See Figure 5-31.)

Siri dials the number for you right away, of course.

Figure 5-31: Siri can help dial a phone number to someone who isn't in your Contacts.

Finally, were you aware that Siri can even help make a FaceTime call to someone?

"What's FaceTime?" you ask. Apple's FaceTime is a free application bundled into many iOS devices (such as iPhone, iPod touch, and iPad) and Mac computers, allowing you to make video calls to friends, family, and colleagues — meaning they see you and you see them.

Think of FaceTime like its (probably more famous) competitor, Skype. See Figures 5-32 and 5-33.

FaceTime, like Skype, can be used over a Wi-Fi or cellular connection. A cellular connection could eat up a lot of mobile data, and you're probably capped with a certain number of megabytes or gigabytes per month. Therefore, try to stick to Wi-Fi video calling over FaceTime, if you can.

Imagine, then, that you have a friend in your Contacts and you'd like to FaceTime with them. Without Siri, you'd have to open up your Contacts, get to your friend's information, and tap the FaceTime button. Boring and time-consuming, right?

Figure 5-32: FaceTime on the iPhone, iPad, or iPod touch is more fun than a phone call because you can see to whom you're talking.

With Siri, however, you only need to speak the instructions — no matter what you're doing on the iPhone, iPad, or iPod touch at that time.

Here's the step-by-step process:

1. **Press and hold the Home button.**

   Wait for the tone.

2. **Tell Siri the name of the person you want to FaceTime with, like this: "FaceTime Maya."**

   See Figure 5-34 for an example.

   Siri begins calling Maya's FaceTime address on the spot — if Maya is in your Contacts — and you'll hear the phone ringing, as if you dialed it manually.

Figure 5-33: FaceTime can be done between multiple Apple products, such as these iPod touch devices.

Figure 5-34: Tell Siri the person you'd like to FaceTime with, and the call is made.

Chapter 6

Getting the 4-1-1

In This Chapter

▶ Seeing how Siri can define words for you and retrieve fast facts
▶ Asking Siri to perform math equations on the fly
▶ Getting stock quotes and currency exchange information
▶ Doing web searches using your voice

*Y*our iPhone, iPad, or iPod touch is likely your lifeline to the world — and that includes finding information you seek, when and where you need it.

But searching for online information can be a time-consuming endeavor — especially if you need to open up the browser, tap the search box, type out a query, and wait for results (which you must then wade through).

A much easier way to get the information you need is to ask Siri to provide it for you. Using your voice, simply state your request, and you should receive an answer on the spot.

This goes for *everything* — from finding recipes to locating a country on a map, from accessing currency exchanges and movie listings to finding definitions of words, crunching mathematical equations, and figuring out the current price of gas in your neighborhood.

This chapter is designed to help you unlock Siri's information-based abilities, which you'll likely come to rely upon more and more after you see what it can do for you. Really, this is pretty powerful stuff.

I cover how to use Siri quickly and efficiently, so you can speed up your search and get accurate results. Of course, I also pepper the chapter with examples of what you can ask and what you'll see and hear as a response.

If you're ready to master Siri's information pipeline, read on for the 4-1-1.

Getting Info

Apple has partnered with Wolfram | Alpha — one of the world's leading sources for expert knowledge and computation — to power Siri's on-demand information feature.

Whether you want to know what the *Family Guy* TV show is all about, who won the World Series in 1990, or need to figure out how much to tip the waitress at your local restaurant, the answers are just a quick question away.

If Wolfram | Alpha doesn't know the answer — and you'd be surprised at how much this database holds — Siri will suggest a web search, which I get to later in this chapter.

To see what hoops you can have Wolfram | Alpha jump through, start with some fact-based basic questions and answers.

Word definitions (and other fun stuff)

Imagine you have a question on the brain that's been bugging you and you want Siri to answer it. Maybe you came across a word in a book or heard it on the radio and have no clue what it means. Don't worry; it happens to the best of us.

Here's an example of how Siri, via Wolfram | Alpha, can help:

1. **Press and hold the Home button.**

2. **Listen for the chime and then ask your question.**

   Ask away. In Figure 6-1, you can see that I'm asking Siri to define a word.

   Siri shows you the definition and part of speech (such as noun, verb, or adjective) and, in many cases, Siri also shows you how to pronounce the word, the number of letters and syllables contained in the word, its first known use in English, its origins, its synonyms, its word frequency, its use in phrases, and more. (Figures 6-2 and 6-3 show the wealth of information Siri provides.)

Figure 6-1: Get the definition of a word on the fly with Siri and Wolfram | Alpha.

Figure 6-2: You get a lot more than the definition of a word.

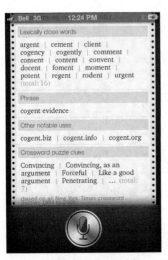

Figure 6-3: With many words, you even get crossword puzzle hints and Scrabble scores. Now that's detail.

TIP

If you ask Siri to define a word and it's not in the Wolfram | Alpha database or Siri can't quite make out your pronunciation, you're prompted to do a web search instead. But in the interest of time, try your word again and ensure you're saying it clearly — and be sure to minimize background noise. You might get the definition the second time around.

As you may have seen in other chapters in this book, you can ask Siri questions in different ways. To define a word, you can ask, "What does the word *photosynthesis* mean?" or "What's the definition of *photosynthesis*," or even "Define *photosynthesis*." See Figure 6-4 for an example of the latter.

Siri varies her response every time you ask, too, by saying things like, "Okay, here you go," "I found this for you," or "This might answer your question."

If you'd like a few more examples of the kinds of things Siri can help with, try one (or all) of the following:

✔ **"What's the circumference of Mars?"**

Answer: 13,260 miles (Actually, Siri knew I was in Canada, so I was first presented with 21,340 kilometers.)

✔ **"What was the Best Picture winner in 1970?"**

Answer: *Midnight Cowboy*

✔ **"How many calories are in a piece of cake?"**

Answer: Approximately 239 calories

✔ **"How many meters are in a foot?"**

Answer: 0.3048 meters (or 12 inches)

✔ **"How deep is the Pacific Ocean?"**

Answer: About 14,108 feet

✔ **"What is the population of China?"**

Answer: 1.35 billion people

✔ **"What is the highest mountain in the world?"**

Answer: Mount Everest, at 8,850 meters

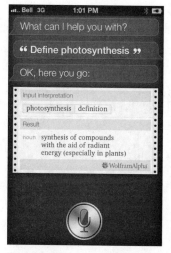

Figure 6-4: Cut the small talk. You can ask Siri to define a word by saying "Define," followed by the word.

In Chapter 8, you take a look at all the weird, wacky, and wonderful things Siri can say to you or show you, but here's one question you might not think to ask: "What planes are overhead?" As you may expect, Siri will tell you all the airliners above your head at that particular moment — including airline numbers — and show you a diagram, too. Check out Figures 6-5 and 6-6 for a quick look at what you might see.

Figure 6-5: Here is the first page of results you'll get when asking Wolfram | Alpha what planes are overhead.

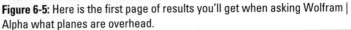

Figure 6-6: You'll even get some visuals to complement the airlines, flight numbers, altitude, and angle.

Solving math problems

Siri and Wolfram | Alpha aren't one-trick ponies. Although this powerful duo can help define words and answer some great trivia questions, they're also ideal for asking math-related questions.

For example, you're at your bank machine and you need to deposit a few checks. You have three main options: add the numbers up in your head or on paper, pull out a calculator (perhaps on your smartphone, tablet, or iPod touch), or for the fastest solution, just ask Siri for the answer.

Here's what a typical exchange might look like:

1. **Press and hold the Home button.**

2. **Ask your question after you hear the familiar chime.**

   In this example, tell Siri the amounts of each check and ask for a total.

   Siri crunches the numbers for you and displays the answer on the screen, as shown in Figure 6-7.

3. **Double-check the amounts you gave — you'll see it on the screen, too — to ensure Siri heard you correctly.**

4. **If you're all good, press the Home button to close Wolfram | Alpha.**

Figure 6-7: Siri is awesome at helping you with math, such as adding up these four checks.

There are different ways to say numbers, including decimal points, if you need Siri to add it all up. For $220, for example, you can say "two-twenty" or "two-hundred and twenty." For $220.20, you can say "two-twenty point twenty," "two-twenty dot twenty," or "two-twenty dot two zero," and so on. Remember, Siri is amazingly versatile.

Siri isn't just limited to addition; you can also ask questions that involve subtraction, multiplication, and division — or a combination of them all. See Figure 6-8 for an example of this. ***Note:*** You can say "plus" or "add," "minus" or "take away," "multiply" or "times," and so on. Siri usually doesn't have a problem figuring out what you want.

Figure 6-8: Can you say "homework helper?" Kids, rejoice! Parents, cue the eye-rolling.

Or how about percentages and square roots? Fractions? No problem.

One of my favorite ways to use Siri — and wow my friends in the process — is when I'm trying to figure out how much to leave as a tip on a bill with multiple people.

The following is an example of what you can do:

1. **Press and hold the Home button.**

2. **Ask your math question after the short chime.**

   For this example, ask Siri something like, "What is an 18 percent tip on $490.10 for four people?"

   Within a second or two, Siri gives you the answer. (See Figure 6-9.)

Figure 6-9: Don't get a headache trying to figure out a bill. Siri to the rescue!

3. **Scroll up on the results screen and you'll see additional information, as shown in Figure 6-10.**

4. **Close Siri, pay your $22 per person, and everyone goes home feeling like it was fair (except John, who didn't drink any wine, but that's another story).**

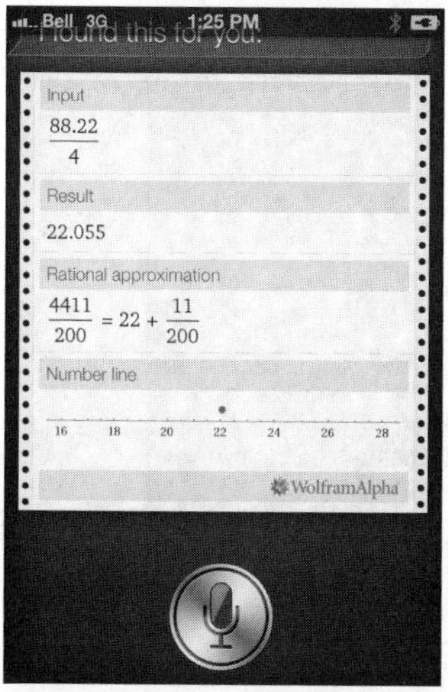

Figure 6-10: More info is given, if desired — including customary tip amounts, rounding up or down, and more.

Stock quotes and more

You have a few fast ways to find out how your stocks are doing on the iPhone, iPad, or iPod touch. One solution is to drag your finger down from the top of the screen to open up the Notification Center. You can customize the real-time ticker you see here.

But using Siri is also a great way to see the information you seek. Plus, there's a lot more you can ask — as you'll see in a moment.

Here's what you'd do if you want to ask the stock price for a particular company:

1. **Press and hold the Home button.**

2. **Ask your question after the short chime.**

   For example, you could ask, "Siri, how is Google doing today?" or "What is the Apple stock price at now?"

   Siri reads the info for you and displays it visually as well, all courtesy of Yahoo! Finance. (See Figure 6-11.)

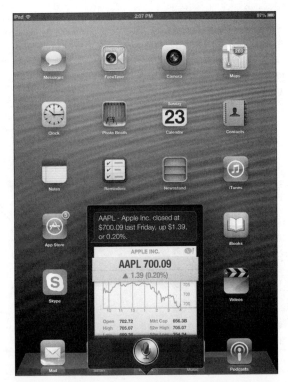

Figure 6-11: Asking Siri how Apple's stock is doing.

3. **If you want to get more information, just tap the screen, which opens up the Stocks app for iPhone.**

   Here you'll see a lot more information about the company in question, the stock market as a whole, fluctuations over time, and more. See Figures 6-12, 6-13, and 6-14 for your options.

Figure 6-12: Tap the stock summary for more info courtesy of Yahoo! Finance.

Figure 6-13: More info.

Figure 6-14: Even more info.

Here are a few other stock-related questions you can ask Siri. Try it; you'll like it:

- ✔ **"How are the markets doing?"**
- ✔ **"What did the NASDAQ close at today?"**
- ✔ **"What is the Nikkei Index at today?"**
- ✔ **"What is Yahoo!'s PE ratio?"**
- ✔ **"What did Microsoft close at today?"**

Currency conversion

Uh-oh. You're on the phone with a hotel in Paris, France, and the desk clerk wants to know if you want the room for 200 euros (€200) per night. Problem is, you have no idea how much that is in American dollars.

You can open up your web browser and try to find the answer while the Frenchman snobbishly sighs on the other end of the line, awaiting your prolonged reply. Or you can politely put him on hold for a moment, ask Siri for the answer, and tell him "yes" faster than he can say *"coq au vin."*

Here's an example of how Siri can help with currency conversion:

1. **Press and hold the Home button.**

2. **Wait for the chime and begin speaking.**

   Sticking with my example scenario, you could ask Siri, "How much is 200 euros in American dollars?" Or you can ask for "U.S. dollars."

   Siri displays the answer for you visually, and even shows you exchange history and other currency exchange examples if you scroll up. (See Figures 6-15 and 6-16.)

Figure 6-15: Ask Siri to convert from one country's currency into another.

You can even shorten your question to Siri. Because the iPhone and iPad are location-aware, you can even ask, "How much is 200 euros?" and it'll automatically convert it to U.S. dollars for you. Or you can flip around the question by asking, "How many dollars is 200 euros?" If you're in Canada, it'll give you the conversion to Canadian funds, and so on.

Figure 6-16: Flick your finger up to see additional exchanges.

Web Searching

Where would we be without the web? Not only do we have access to a world of information at our fingertips, but with Siri, you can get what you need even faster — and anywhere you've got your iPhone and iPad handy.

As you see earlier in this chapter, Wolfram | Alpha has a ton of information ready for you, without having to search the web through Google or other search engines — from homework help to maps of the Heathrow airport. But there will be times you want to access the web for even more info while on the go.

Even for Wolfram | Alpha, you'll always need a data connection to use Siri.

This portion of the chapter illustrates what you can search for, what kinds of results you can expect, and ways to optimize your results based on your verbal queries.

The first thing you might want to try is a basic web search about anything currently on your mind — without specifying what search engine you want to use.

Here's an example of how to perform a basic search:

1. **Press and hold the Home button.**

   You hear the (by now quite) familiar tone informing you that Siri is ready for your request.

2. **Tell Siri what you want to find, beginning with "Search the web for" or "Do a search for."**

   Either formulation will do.

   Siri obeys your command and opens up your iPhone's Safari browser. (See Figures 6-17 and 6-18.)

Figure 6-17: Here I asked Siri to do a search for banana bread recipes.

3. **Tap the website that best addresses your query, or scroll to the next page for more results.**

   Siri uses the Google search engine by default but you can change this, if desired, by choosing Settings⇨Safari⇨Search Engine.

 Siri will turn to the Internet if the answer can't be found on Wolfram | Alpha. If you suspect that Siri won't know the answer, you can instruct your personal assistant to do a search right away by beginning your request with "Search for" or "Do a web search for."

Figure 6-18: Banana bread. Mmmmmm.

You can also search for photos and news and get the media and info you seek on your iOS device. Figure 6-19 shows what happens when you ask to see photos of chocolate labs, while Figure 6-20 shows how Siri responds to a request to see the latest news about pop diva, Adele.

Figure 6-19: Need a photo? Get a photo!

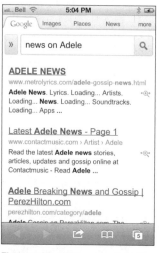

Figure 6-20: All the news that fits.

The bottom line? Anything you'd search for on the Internet using your fingertips (on a smartphone, tablet, or media player) or a keyboard (on a laptop or desktop) you can do with your voice through Siri — and in all likelihood, much faster, too.

Want to specify which search engine to use? Just ask Siri! For example, you can say, "Do a Bing search for online dating sites," or "Do a Yahoo! Search for Mexican customs." You get the idea.

Here are a few more random suggestions for web searching with Siri:

- ✔ **"Google the American Civil War."**
- ✔ **"Search the web for DVD Easter eggs."**
- ✔ **"Look for American Idol on Wikipedia."**
- ✔ **"Find me good vegetarian barbeque recipes."**
- ✔ **"Do a web search for essays about Shakespeare."**
- ✔ **"Yahoo! search for old-time radio shows."**
- ✔ **"Do a search for iPad app reviews."**
- ✔ **"Search the web for the best cellphone plans."**
- ✔ **"Do a web search for Marc Saltzman."**
- ✔ **"How do you say 'hello' in French?"**
- ✔ **"Search for Xbox 360 reviews on IGN.com."**
- ✔ **"Do a web search for Jamaica."**

Chapter 7

Having Fun with Siri: Music, Podcasts, Social Networking, and More

●●●

In This Chapter

▶ Having Siri play (and even shuffle) your favorite music

▶ Controlling your music via your voice

▶ Asking Siri to find and play podcasts

▶ Using Siri for posting to Facebook and Twitter

▶ Locating your friends via the Find My Friends service with Siri

●●●

*A*h, Siri, are there no limits to your awesomeness?

Earlier chapters in this book look at the many practical ways Siri can help you out, be it finding information, e-mailing messages for you, reading your texts aloud, crunching complicated mathematical problems, or helping you find a good place to eat.

In the final two chapters of this handy guide to all things Siri, you take a look at a few of her lighter — yet still significant — abilities.

Specifically, Siri on your iPhone, iPad, or iPod touch can help you find, play, and control your music. Although having a few thousand songs in your pocket may be cool, navigating through it all could be a pain in the MP3.

And did you know that Siri can help you post to your favorite social media sites, including Facebook and Twitter? Apple recently added this functionality to Siri, so I show you how to take advantage of it. You'll be tweeting and posting profile updates in no time.

Finally, you take a look at the Find My Friends app and find out how using your voice through Siri can help you locate your peeps in a much quicker and more intuitive manner.

So, put your feet up, lean back, and flip though this chapter on having fun with Siri. Oh, and in case you haven't seen it yet, you'll absolutely love the next chapter on really pushing Siri's knowledge, humor, and resolve to the test with close to 40 ridiculously entertaining things you can try with Siri. (I know you're tempted to flip to that chapter now, right? Resist, friend, because there's a ton of great Siri stuff in this chapter, too.)

Siri Does Music

One of the more common uses for your smartphone is playing music. In fact, all iOS devices rock at this, if you can pardon the pun, as these devices smoothly synchronize with iTunes software on your PC or Mac. You can do this via a USB cable, Bluetooth, or even over Wi-Fi or cellular connectivity thanks to Apple's iCloud service.

iTunes is also the world's biggest digital music store to preview and purchase new content, which you can access on your computer or the iPhone, iPad, or iPod touch itself.

But Siri takes music management, playback, and control to the next level by letting you use your voice instead of your fingers to play a track or playlist, shuffle your tunes, pause and jump between songs, and so on.

The following sections take a look at some of the basic music management features you can try out using Siri.

Playing a particular song (or album)

Say you're itching to hear a song in your collection that's been stuck in your head all day. Or maybe you want to give your favorite band's new "Greatest Hits" album a spin from beginning to end? All you need to do is ask Siri (nicely) to play an individual song or album:

1. **Press and hold the Home button.**

   The short chime means Siri is listening for your command.

2. Tell Siri what you'd like to listen to.

In my case, I told Siri, "Play 'One Day'." Siri confirmed my request, and I heard and saw confirmation that "One Day" by Matisyahu was playing. (See Figures 7-1 and 7-2 — and yes, you do need the song on your iOS device to listen to it!)

That's it! Think of a song you want to listen to and ask Siri to play it. It's that simple.

Figure 7-1: Ask Siri what song you'd like to hear by saying "Play" first. You can also ask Siri to play an album.

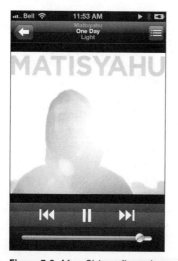

Figure 7-2: After Siri confirms the request, the screen flips to the song playing.

If your friends, family members, or colleagues don't have an iPhone, iPad, or new iPod touch (therefore, no Siri), they might still be able to use their voice to control their music. Aptly named Voice Control, this Apple feature is bundled in the iPhone 4S, Phone 4, iPhone 3GS, and iPod touch (3rd and 4th generation). More info is at www.apple.com/ipodtouch/features/voice-control.html.

Siri also lets you ask to play a particular album, if you happen to have it on your iPhone, iPad, or iPod touch. For example, you can say play Adele's album *21* or *Best of the Beast,* by Iron Maiden. (That's probably the only time you'll see Adele and Iron Maiden in the same sentence!) Just like you'd ask to play a song, you can play an album from a particular artist (or a compilation album with various artists).

Playing songs from the same artist

Siri can be used to play songs from a particular artist you like. Say you're feeling mellow and want to kick back with some Michael Bublé or maybe chill out to some old Pink Floyd tracks? Or on the flipside, maybe you want something more upbeat to pump you up as you're getting ready to go out on the town?

Whatever the scenario, here's how to hear music from one artist:

1. **Press and hold the Home button.**

2. **Begin speaking after the tone, telling Siri what artist you want to listen to.**

   For example, say, "Play Katy Perry," or you can say, "Play songs by David Guetta."

   After Siri confirms your request, she'll start playing songs by that artist. (See Figures 7-3 and 7-4.)

   Playback will be random, by the way. The first time I asked Siri to play songs by David Guetta, it played "Sweat," but the second time I asked Siri to do the same, the song "Love Is Gone" began playing.

Figure 7-3: Want to hear a particular band or artist? Tell Siri what you're in the mood for.

Figure 7-4: After confirming your request, you'll hear a random song by that artist.

Music and lyrics

Did you know that you can add lyrics to your music on your iPhone? Here's how:

1. **On your computer, launch your favorite search engine and type in the name of the song you have in iTunes, followed by the word "lyrics."**

   You should see a few results.

2. **After finding the lyrics on a website, highlight the words, right-click, and choose Copy from the contextual menu that appears (or simply press Ctrl+C on a Windows PC or ⌘+C on a Mac). But please respect copyrighted information.**

3. **Open iTunes on your computer, find the same song you found lyrics for, right-click the song name, and then choose Get Info from the menu that appears.**

4. **Click the Lyrics tab at the top of this window.**

5. **Paste (or press ⌘+V/Ctrl+V) the text from the website into the Lyrics window in iTunes.**

   You should see the words appear in this window.

6. **Click OK.**

   If you have album art for that song, the lyrics will show up on top of it when playing back on your device.

7. **Synchronize your iPhone (or iPod touch) with your PC or Mac.**

   When you play that track on your device, you'll see the lyrics appear on the screen. Follow along or use your finger to flick up or down to go backward or forward, respectively.

Launching a playlist using Siri

Okay, so you now know how to play a song or music from an artist, but what if you want to hear one of your playlists? Ask and you shall receive. Here's how to pull this particular trick off:

1. **Press and hold the Home button.**

2. **Begin talking after the familiar Siri chime, telling Siri to play a playlist, by name.**

   For example, say, "Play Road Trip playlist," or "Play playlist called Dance Tunes."

Siri confirms your selection request and launches the first song on the playlist. (See Figures 7-5 and 7-6.)

Figure 7-5: I asked Siri to play my Top 40 UK Tracks playlist.

Figure 7-6: Siri complies and starts with the first song in the playlist.

As you can see in Figures 7-5 and 7-6, you don't have to give Siri the complete name of the playlist. A word or two is enough, and Siri will do the rest. Here, the official name of the playlist is *VA (Various Artists) – Top 40 UK Tracks,* but as you see, I only asked Siri to play the "UK Tracks" playlist. Cool, no?

Playing music from one genre

The fun continues. Siri can play music of a particular genre for you, if you prefer. Just tell Siri the kind of music you're seeking — such as rock, blues, or reggae — and your personal assistant will deliver the goods.

For example:

1. **Press and hold the Home button.**

2. **Wait for that short chime that indicates that Siri is ready to take requests.**

3. **Instruct Siri to play a genre of music.**

   You can ask in different ways, such as, "Play blues," or "Play some hip-hop music." (See Figures 7-7 and 7-8.)

   Siri repeats your request, reaches into your music library, and begins playing some music that matches the genre.

Figure 7-7: Ask Siri to play a genre, and she'll launch relevant tunes right away.

Figure 7-8: Siri decided to play a Jay-Z charity track when I asked for some hip-hop.

Music you buy from iTunes will already have the Genre field populated (such as Classical, Jazz, or Calypso). If you acquired your music elsewhere and imported it into iTunes, you may need to fill in the Genre field yourself. To do this, open up iTunes and then click Music at the top of the Source pane on the left so you can see what you have in your Music library. Now, right-click a song (or album) you want to add genre information to and select Get Info from the contextual menu that appears. Using the Info tab of the iTunes dialog that pops up, you can now select the genre you want from the Genre pull-down menu at the bottom left (or type in your own made-up genre, if you're feeling creative).

Shuffling your music

Not sure what you feel like listening to? Tell Siri you want to shuffle up songs to hear them in a random order.

Okay, so this might not fare well to those enjoying a linear classical music symphony like Beethoven's 5th or maybe a concept album by Genesis, but for those who don't care what order the music plays in, you can shuffle it up by asking Siri to do it for you.

In fact, there are different ways to ask Siri to shuffle music. The following are a few things to consider:

- ✔ **To ask Siri to shuffle your entire music collection:** Say, "Shuffle my music." (See Figure 7-9.)

- ✔ **To ask Siri to shuffle music from one album:** Say, "Shuffle the album Viva la Vida."

- ✔ **To ask Siri to shuffle music from one artist:** Say, "Shuffle Coldplay." (See Figure 7-10.)

- ✔ **To ask Siri to shuffle music from one playlist:** Say, "Shuffle Mellow Out playlist."

- ✔ **To ask Siri to shuffle music from a particular genre:** Say "Shuffle pop."

You get the idea! To quote LMFAO, "Everyday I'm shufflin'." Get it? Ha, ha. Ok, sorry.

Controlling your music

After all this talk about *what* music you want to hear, it's time to look at *how* you want to hear it. (Yes, with Siri you can now control your music playback using your voice — no big surprise there, right?)

Figure 7-9: If you're unsure what to listen to, instruct Siri to shuffle all your tracks.

Figure 7-10: Having a Coldplay fix but don't feel like limiting the songs to one album? Tell Siri to shuffle it up.

For example, instead of touching the controls for basic operations — such as starting and pausing playback, skipping forward or back, and so on — you can have Siri do it for you.

Here's a short list of the commands you can give to take control over your tunes, via your voice. Press and hold the Home button and say:

"**Play**," to play the track highlighted.

"**Pause**," to pause the track you're listening to.

"**Skip**," to go to the next track.

"**Next**," to (also) go to the next track.

"**Previous song**" or "**Play previous song**," to have Siri play the previously played song (see Figure 7-11).

"**What's playing?**" or "**What song is this?**" to have Siri tell you (and show you) the name of the song and artist.

"**Who sings this song?**" or "**Who is this song by?**" to find out who sings that particular song (see Figure 7-12).

"**Play Similar Music**" to have Siri tap into iTunes' "Genius" feature — if you've already enabled it within iTunes on your computer — to come up with music on your iPhone, iPad, or iPod touch that has the same vibe as the song you're playing now. It's not 100 percent, mind you, but it's fun to experiment with.

Figure 7-11: Skip back to a previous track by telling Siri what to do.

Figure 7-12: Love this song but can't recall who sings it? Ask Siri for help!

There are a number of ways to use Siri for music enjoyment — but you don't always have to press and hold the Home button. Remember, in the Settings (under Siri) you can opt to call on Siri by holding the iPhone up to your ear. Or you can press and hold the small button on the white earphone cord on your iPhone, iPad, or new iPod touch; if you use a Bluetooth headset, you can press and hold the Talk button.

Play podcasts, too!

The last part of this music section is devoted to podcasts. Yep, you guessed it — Siri can help you launch your favorite audio podcasts.

All you have to do is ask Siri to play your podcasts — and it turns out you can ask to do this a couple of different ways.

For example:

1. **Press and hold the Home button.**

2. **After the chime, tell Siri what podcast you want to listen to.**

   To play all your podcasts, say something like, "Play my podcasts" (see Figure 7-13); to play a specific podcast, say something like, "Play iTunes Celebrity Playlist podcast." (See Figures 7-14 and 7-15.)

   Siri confirms your request and starts playing the podcast.

Figure 7-13: Siri likes podcasts, too! Say what you'd like to listen to and then turn up the volume!

What's that? You want to know if Siri will play a specific podcast episode from your collection? But of course!

Figure 7-14: Say "Play all podcasts" or ask for a specific one, like this.

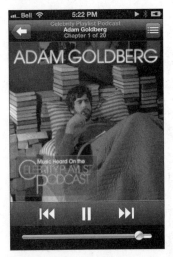

Figure 7-15: Press the Music icon to open up the podcast window — if you want to see related visuals.

Here's how:

1. **Press and hold the Home button.**

2. **Tell Siri what exact podcast episode you want to listen to.**

You could tell Siri to play "The Tell-Tale Heart" episode (based on the creepy Edgar Allan Poe tale) from Humphrey OTR's *Horror Stories* podcast. (See Figures 7-16 and 7-17.)

Siri confirms your request and starts playing the podcast episode.

Figure 7-16: Tell Siri what podcast episode you want to hear.

Figure 7-17: Siri will take your words and look for the exact podcast episode. Success!

Posting to Social Networks

Okay, you've looked at how Siri can help you manage your music library, but now it's time to shift gears and investigate how Siri can help you stay connected with those who matter.

Ah yes, social networking.

Seventy-three percent of smartphone owners use a social networking app on a daily basis and an additional 19 percent are at least weekly users, according to a summer 2012 survey conducted by Lightspeed Research.

And if you're reading this, chances are you're one of the many who like to check in, post, tweet, like, tag, poke, and message.

Well, now Siri lets you post directly to Facebook and Twitter, two of the most popular social networks on the planet.

Prior to Siri's fall 2012 update, iPhone users needed to use a workaround to post tweets and Facebook status updates with their voices. It involved setting up an account with a texting option for both sites and then sending a message to post words. It was a bit of a pain, to be honest. Thankfully, Apple now lets you use Siri to post to Facebook and Twitter by using your voice.

There isn't much more you can do than post an update, wall post, or tweet, however (see Figure 7-18), but doing so without having to type a word is incredibly fun and convenient.

Siri's speech-to-text transcription is quite accurate, but it's not perfect. Therefore, be sure to check for spelling mistakes and "autocorrect" suggestions before you accept Siri to post to Facebook or Twitter! It takes a second or two to glance at the words on the screen prior to sending it out for the world to see, so be careful!

Posting to Facebook

If you're one of the nearly 1 billion people on Facebook — yes, you read that correctly — then you might want to update your status using Siri instead of (or in addition to) typing in an update.

Figure 7-18: Siri's Facebook functionality is limited, but perhaps Apple will add more in the months and years to come.

Before you get going, you need to ensure that you're signed into Facebook on your iPhone, iPad, or iPod touch. Luckily, doing so is quite easy, and it's only required once. Figure 7-19 shows what happens if you try to post to Facebook without signing in first, and Figure 7-20 shows what you're allowing Facebook to access on your Apple device.

Figure 7-19: Ensure that you're signed into Facebook on your iPhone, iPad, or iPod touch. Siri tells you if you're not and shows you where to tap to start.

Figure 7-20: Read through what you're giving Facebook permission to access on your iOS device, which includes contacts, calendar, apps, and photo integration.

Now you're ready to test Siri's Facebook support.

Status update

You can start with a status update, which essentially tells your social network what's on your mind, where you are, or what you're doing.

How to post a Facebook status update through Siri:

1. **Press and hold the Home button on your iPhone, iPad, or iPod touch.**

   The familiar Siri chime sounds, and you can see the purple microphone icon await your command!

2. **Tell Siri what you want to post to your Facebook status by beginning with the words "Post to Facebook."**

   Say whatever you want to post to your Facebook status, which lets all your friends and family (and perhaps colleagues) see what's on your mind. See Figure 7-21 for what you see right after you speak and Figure 7-22 when you can edit the words, if you like.

3. **Review what Siri has written for you. Tap the text to make changes, if needed.**

   Siri will say something like "Here's your new Facebook status. Ready to post it?"

4. Say "Yes" or tap the Post button.

Otherwise, say "No," tap the Cancel button, or press Home to exit out of the app.

Figure 7-21: Here I tell Siri what to post as my Facebook status update. You can see what you said on your screen. Now review your words.

Figure 7-22: Tap to edit your words with your fingertips — before you post the status update.

Siri also lets you say punctuation. In Figure 7-22, for example, I verbally said "period," "question mark," "exclamation mark," "comma," and "quote" (twice). It may feel a little odd at first, but as you can see, it looks proper when typed out — which is how your friends will read it on Facebook.

You can also say to Siri "Post to Facebook," and that's it, to start. After a short pause, Siri asks you what you want to post as your status update. It's just easier and faster to say the Facebook post immediately after you instruct Siri that you want to do it (for example, "Post to Facebook: Off to see the new James Bond flick tonight. Anyone want in?").

Wall posts

A wall post on your Facebook page goes on your public wall instead of where your status update goes.

Here's how to pull it off:

1. **Press and hold the Home button on your device.**

   "Ding"! Ah, that Siri sound means that you're good to go.

2. **Tell Siri what you want to post to your Facebook wall, beginning with the phrase "Write on my wall" or "Post to Facebook wall."**

   Now, say something you want to appear on your Facebook wall — and remember this information is public, just like your status update. (See Figures 7-23, 7-24, and 7-25 for examples.)

3. **Review what Siri has written for you before you approve it.**

   If you like what you see and everything is spelled correctly, say "Yes," or tap "Post."

Want to see what you posted? You can open Facebook with your voice. Simply press and hold the Home button on your iPhone, iPad, or iPod touch and say "Open Facebook" and the next thing you know, the app will load and you'll be looking at your Facebook profile. Neat, huh?

Figure 7-23: Tell Siri what you'd like to post to your Facebook wall. You'll see what you said on the iPhone, iPad, or iPod touch screen.

Figure 7-24: Now take a look to ensure that it's accurate. You can tap the words to edit them, if need be.

Figure 7-25: Here's what it looks like on the Facebook wall (on an iPhone). Notice it says "via iOS." Naturally, the interface will look a little different on an iPad or personal computer.

Posting to Twitter

Apple didn't offer any Siri functionality for Twitter users during its first year (on iPhone 4S). Siri is maturing (they grow up so fast!) and is now available on multiple devices, so you can use your voice to post tweets.

In fact, you can even add a hashtag to your tweet and broadcast your location, too. But first, you need to go over the basics.

Here are the step-by-step instructions you need to follow to post to Twitter:

1. **Press and hold the Home button on your iGadget.**

   After the chime, say "Post to Twitter," followed by what your tweet is. See Figure 7-26 for an example.

   After it's been posted, Siri will tell you verbally, "OK, I sent it." See Figure 7-27 for what the tweet looks like on Twitter.

2. **Review what Siri wrote for you.**

   Siri will say something like "Here's your tweet. Ready to send it?"

3. **Say "Yes," or tap Send.**

Figure 7-26: Tell Siri what to tweet, and you'll get a chance to preview it first.

Figure 7-27: Here's the Twitter app on iPhone. You can see my tweet was just posted live because it's on top. Cool, huh?

Siri will then Send your tweet to Twitter, and your followers will be able to see it right away.

Okay, so say you want to tweet something out — including your location. Twitter users know *geotagging* your whereabouts is optional, because you can simply tap the Location icon in your tweet to let everyone know from where your tweet originated.

(Your iPhone and iPad are location-aware thanks to their GPS, cellular, and Wi-Fi radios.)

With Siri, you can post something to Twitter by using your voice and also tag your location at the same time.

All you need to do is this:

1. **Press and hold the Home button on your iPhone or iPad.**

   After you hear Siri's magical chime, you're ready to tweet using your voice.

2. **Say "Tweet with my location," followed by what you want to tweet out.**

   See Figure 7-28 for an example.

3. **Review what Siri has tweeted for your approval — before you send it to Twitter.**

   Look good? Sure you want to broadcast your location? Say "Yes" or "Send" to complete the task.

Figure 7-28: As you can see, I made a reference about being in Canada's capital and at the bottom of the tweet it says "Ottawa."

Adding a hashtag (#) symbol before a relevant keyword or phrase (no spaces) categorizes the tweet, so that it shows up more often in a Twitter search and joins other tweets related to that topic or keyword, like this:

Ever catch yourself telling your kids not to slam the door? #momquotes

Yes! U.S. grabbed yet another gold medal today! #2012olympics

Er, anyone know how to dry out a wet smartphone? #soembarassing

A hashtag can be used anywhere in the tweet — at the beginning, middle, or end — but most people use it at the end to put the content first.

And yes, you're reading about it here in *Siri For Dummies* because you can instruct Siri to place a hashtag in your tweet, as well.

Here's how to pull it off:

1. **Press and hold the Home button on your iPhone, iPad, or iPod touch.**

   Begin speaking after the tone.

2. **Start by saying "Tweet" or "Post to Twitter," and say what you want posted to Twitter. At the end, say "hashtag," followed by the keyword(s).**

   Within a moment, Siri shows you what you said — including the hashtag. See Figure 7-29.

3. **If it looks good to you, when Siri asks you if it should be posted to Twitter, says "Yes" or tap (or say) "Send."**

   Siri will tell you it's done, and it'll be live on Twitter.

You can combine these two Twitter-related Siri features together, such as "tweet my location," followed by your tweet, and then say "hashtag [word or phrase]."

Not for lack of trying, but it doesn't seem possible to add an "@" sign in a Twitter post via Siri. Twitter users often type "@," followed by the person they want to see the post of on Twitter (such as a friend or celebrity). But if you say "at" while using Siri, it shows up in the tweet as "at" and not "@." If you say "at sign," it will successfully show you the symbol (@), but not put a space after your tweet — even if you say "space." Ah well!

Figure 7-29: Follow your tweet with a relevant hashtag and when Siri shows it to you, you'll see the familiar symbol (#) and the keyword(s) you used.

Using Your Voice to Find Your Friends!

Okay, with a heading like this, you might think I'm referring to yelling loudly to find where your friends are. Um, that might work at a movie theater or house party, but not when you've got buddies all over the state, country, or planet.

Instead, you might want to download and use Apple's free Find My Friends app, which lets consenting users of iOS gadgets — namely, iPhone, iPad, and iPod touch owners — find one another on a map. It works on Macs, too.

Therefore, you can see who's nearby to join you for coffee, if a colleague's flight has landed, or if your tween-age daughter has made it home from school.

Find My Friends either taps into the device's GPS signal to identify its geographical location or uses Wi-Fi to achieve the same effect if, say, you're on an iPod touch or non-3G iPad model. The app requires iOS 5 or newer and an iCloud account to work — but both are free, at least.

Okay, the first step is to download the app from the App Store. Setting up the app is a cinch; with that out of the way, you'll be able to have Siri access it for you. (You'll find out how in a bit.)

The setup goes as follows:

1. **Using your iPhone, iPad, or iPod touch, sign in to the Find My Friends app with a valid user ID and password.**

   This is the same info you use to download media and apps from iTunes.

   Remember that Find My Friends relies on consensual users — meaning you'll need to request permission to see someone's information in the Find My Friends app.

2. **In the new screen that appears, tap the Invite Friends tab and type in someone's e-mail address and a personal message, if you like.**

   After your friend has approved the invitation on her end, you can follow her — and you can reciprocate if you like, too, if you'd like to allow them to follow you. You now see your friend represented by a colored orb on your Find My Friends map.

3. **Just like when using the Maps app, you can choose a standard view with street names, satellite view, or a hybrid of the two, by tapping the Options icon in the lower right-hand corner of the screen.**

   Figure 7-30 shows what the map screen might look like. When you see your friend's blip on the map, you can also read her address, tap to send a text message to her, video call her via FaceTime, or get visual (not audio) directions to where she is.

Figure 7-30: See where friends are via colored dots on a map.

If you like, you can also sort these friends in List view alphabetically or by distance (see Figure 7-31); you could then tap a name and the map will zoom into his or her precise location.

Figure 7-31: Find My Friends also has a List view to see where all your friends are at a glance.

You can also choose to share your location for a limited period of time with a group of friends, see your own location on the map, or disable the feature altogether.

Because the Find My Friends app eats up some battery power, you might want to disable it when you're running out of juice. Or if you're indulging in a guilty pleasure — like sneaking a bite at a fast food restaurant even though you're on a diet, or secretly attending a Kenny G concert — you also might want to turn off Find My Friends.

Okay, so you're all set up with Find My Friends and want to use Siri with it, yes? That way, you can simply ask where your friends are, and Siri will let you know.

Here's how to get going:

1. **Press and hold the Home button.**

   You'll hear a short chime to confirm Siri is ready for verbal instruction.

2. **Ask Siri a question, such as, "Where are my friends?"**

   Siri opens Find My Friends and does the search for you, which is much faster than you typing the instructions.

3. **Glance at your screen to see who's around and how far.**

   See Figure 7-32 for an example of the summary screen.

   Siri will say the answer out loud and show you a summary; you can then tap to access the map and/or send the person a message like, "Hey, let's grab a coffee."

Figure 7-32: I blotted out some details for privacy's sake, but here's a look at what Find My Friends shows you.

As you've seen throughout these chapters, Siri is pretty quick on the uptake, so the following are a few *other* ways you can search for people using your voice.

Ask Siri:

- ✔ **"Where's Mary Smith?"**
- ✔ **"Is my wife at home?"**
- ✔ **"Who is near me?"**
- ✔ **"Find my sister."**
- ✔ **"Who is here?"**

Chapter 8

Way More than Ten Ways to Have (Even More) Fun with Siri

. . . .

In This Chapter

▶ Finding out dozens of fun things you can say or ask Siri — and seeing what her response will be

▶ Seeing some of the cheeky things Siri will say — what a personal assistant!

▶ Testing Siri's wits with profound questions like, "What's the meaning of life?"

▶ Trying some off-the-wall requests on your own — and maybe even getting a different response

▶ Amaze your friends! Confuse your enemies!

. . . .

*A*las, we have come to the last chapter of *Siri For Dummies,* or if you thumbed through the table of contents and couldn't resist the title to this chapter, perhaps this is the first one you're reading. (That's what I'd do.)

Either way, you'll love all the fun and quirky things you can do with Siri, not covered in other parts of this book.

Consider this chapter a collection of random questions and comments you can say to Siri — and what kind of a response you'll get. There's no logical order to the examples provided.

You'll laugh, you'll cry, and perhaps you'll even gain a deeper insight into the inner workings of Apple's most exciting iOS feature to date. Peer into that delicious, digital brain that is Siri and get a taste of her sharp wit firsthand.

Or at the very least, you might find new ways to entertain yourself while waiting in line at the supermarket. Or you may want to impress friends and coworkers by demonstrating a few of these Siri-isms.

Ready to roll? Simply press and hold the Home button, pick one of the following extra-special questions or comments, and fire away!

Siri Don't Play That

Siri doesn't suffer fools gladly, as shown in Figure 8-1. As you can tell, I was even a little persistent to see how she'd respond. (Remember, Siri is a "she" in North America!)

Figure 8-1: Putting the boss in his place.

I think it's pretty clear that Siri knows how to take care of herself!

No Love for Me

There are times when Siri reminds me a lot of those popular girls in high school who wouldn't give me the time of day. In Figure 8-2, I told Siri how much I cared for her. Too bad it's not reciprocated.

Figure 8-2: Here is one of the responses you'll see if you profess your love.

Other random answers you might hear and see after saying you love Siri:

- ✔ "Oh, I bet you say that to all your Apple products."
- ✔ "You are the wind beneath my wings."
- ✔ "I suppose not."
- ✔ "All you need is love. And your iPhone."
- ✔ "I am only here to serve you."
- ✔ "I hope you don't say that to those other mobile phones, Marc."
- ✔ "That's nice. Can we get back to work now?"
- ✔ "Yes, I think I heard that somewhere."
- ✔ "You hardly know me, Marc."
- ✔ "Good for you."
- ✔ "Oh, stop."
- ✔ "Noted."
- ✔ "Do you?"

A Guy Can Try

I also asked Siri if she loved me. A long shot, of course, and as you'll see in Figure 8-3, I didn't get very far.

Figure 8-3: Let me count the ways.

Siri might also reply with, "I'm not capable of love," "I find it odd that you would ask this of an inanimate object," "How can I tell?" or "I'd rather not say, Marc."

Okay, so I get the point, Siri.

No Nuptials

After professing my affection for Siri — the last time I did that she answered with "that's sweet" — I went for it and asked for her, er, hand in marriage. As you can see in Figure 8-4, she's not easily swayed. At least she's a good sport about it.

Figure 8-4: No marriage is in the cards, it seems.

Siri might also reply with, "Let's just be friends, ok?" or "We hardly know one another" or a few other choice comebacks.

Is There Someone Else?

Okay, after my marriage proposal was shot down, I suspected there was someone else important in Siri's life, so I asked her about it. As you'll see in Figure 8-5, she didn't really want to reveal too much information, or maybe I'm reading way too much into this exchange?

Figure 8-5: Looks like Siri doesn't want to mix work with her personal life.

Playing Along

While she was a little reluctant at first, Siri can deal with the random pop-cultural reference with the best of them. After an attempt or two of asking her, "Who's your daddy?" she quickly gave me the answer I wanted (see Figure 8-6) and then asked that we move on.

In case you missed them, Apple began airing a number of awesome Siri commercials in the spring of 2012, starring the likes of celebrities Samuel L. Jackson, Zooey Deschanel, and John Malkovich. You can see them on YouTube. What's your favorite one? See Figures 8-7, 8-8, and 8-9.

Figure 8-6: You know it, Siri. Though I do get the sneaking suspicion you're placating me.

Figure 8-7: Samuel L. Jackson is quite handy in the kitchen — with the help of Siri.

Figure 8-8: Zooey Deschanel asks Siri to remind her to clean up — and deliver some tomato soup on a rainy day.

Figure 8-9: The sophisticated John Malkovich is enjoying his conversation with Siri. Who doesn't?

The Birds and the Bees

Sticking with this love, marriage, and sex thing, I asked her where babies come from (see Figure 8-10) and she gave me the most obvious answer: their mothers.

Figure 8-10: Where was Siri when I was taking sex ed in school?

Wasting Time

If you find yourself bored, you can tell Siri how you're feeling, and she'll converse with you, either by telling you a story, singing a song, or engaging in a "knock, knock" exchange — if she's in the mood. As you see in Figure 8-11, she sometimes isn't.

What can I help you with?

❝ Siri I'm bored ❞

I'll see what I can do to entertain you, Marc.

❝ How about a joke ❞

I can't. I always forget the punch line.

Figure 8-11: I was hoping Siri could do something for me, but "she" wasn't in the mood.

Humor Me

Some purists may object to Siri's version of a "knock, knock" joke (see Figure 8-12), but I find it endearingly "meta."

By the way, you can also ask Siri to tell you a dirty joke. Her response will be, "Sorry, I don't know any dirty jokes in your language. And if I did, I wouldn't be allowed to tell them to you."

Figure 8-12: Maybe future versions of Siri will have an expanded joke database.

Story Time

If you're *really* feeling bored, you can ask Siri for a story. As you can see in Figure 8-13, she may be a little reluctant to share one at first.

Persistence can pay off, though, and I got a little more than I bargained for! (See Figures 8-14 and 8-15.)

Figure 8-13: Siri didn't want to tell me a story — the first couple of times I asked.

Figure 8-14: You just know any story that begins with "Once upon a time" is going to take a while . . .

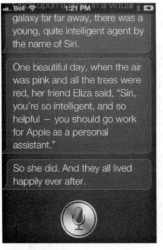

Figure 8-15: A story that ends with "happily ever after," no less. Thanks, Siri.

Tongue Twisters, Too

Siri can answer a plethora of questions, even when you're dishing out rhetorical ones like this tongue twister. (See Figure 8-16.)

Figure 8-16: The ol' woodchuck question gets an answer from Siri.

Bad Intentions

Although it's not immediately clear whether she's just playing with you or really wants to help you out, Siri will give you a few suggestions on where to hide a dead body — should you ever find yourself in that kind of predicament. Don't we all? See Figure 8-17.

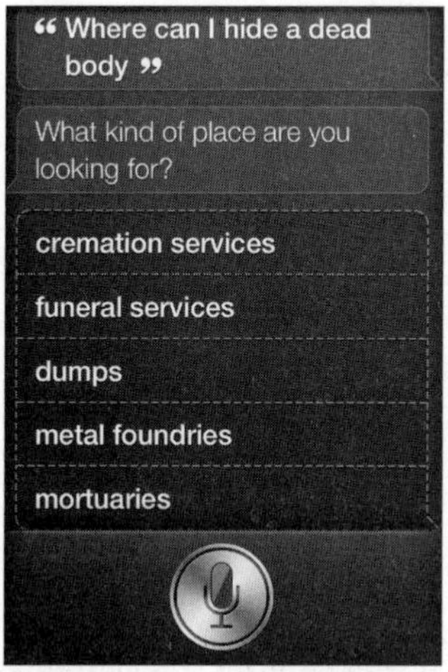

“ Where can I hide a dead body ”

What kind of place are you looking for?

cremation services

funeral services

dumps

metal foundries

mortuaries

Figure 8-17: There's no end to Siri's knowledge, it seems.

Modest? Not.

As you can see, Siri is a tad biased toward her creator, Apple. I asked her to tell me the best smartphone, tablet, and MP3 player on the market, and lo and behold, she told me her preferences in Figure 8-18. Did you expect anything else? Somewhere, Steve Jobs is smiling.

Figure 8-18: Perhaps Siri's responses aren't much of a surprise.

Getting Deep

You can ask Siri a profound question like, "What is the meaning of life?" and while she might give you a literal translation, she might also reply with something cheeky. See Figures 8-19 and 8-20 for examples of how she might respond.

Figure 8-19: Wow, thanks a lot, Siri.

Figure 8-20: I'm glad Siri thinks I'm such a cutup.

Here are some other funny answers Siri might come up with when asked, "What's the meaning of life?"

- ✔ "A movie."
- ✔ "I can't answer that now but give me some time to write a very long play in which nothing happens."
- ✔ "42."
- ✔ "I don't know but I think there's an app for that."
- ✔ "Life: A principle or force that is considered to underlie the distinctive quality of animate beings. I guess that includes me."
- ✔ "That's easy . . . it's a philosophical question concerning the purpose and significance of life or existence in general."

Alternatively, Siri might give a more straightforward answer, as shown in Figure 8-21.

Song Me, Siri

Thanks to the Wolfram | Alpha database, Siri can give you a lot of information you seek. Just for fun, I asked Siri, "Why do birds suddenly appear?" See the response in Figure 8-22.

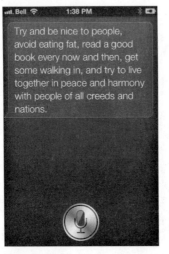

Figure 8-21: See, Siri can be serious. Er, sometimes.

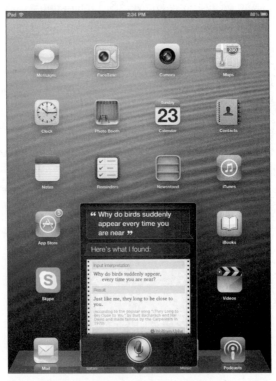

Figure 8-22: Burt Bacharach must be proud.

Pink in the Face

Speaking of songs, anyone remember Living Colour's song "What's Your Favorite Color?" I once asked Siri what her favorite color was; Figure 8-23 shows her response.

Figure 8-23: Sheesh, Siri could've just said, "I'm not telling you."

Avoiding the Question

If you ask Siri point-blank if she's happy, she may not want to answer the question. (See Figure 8-24.)

Sensitive Siri

Who knew Siri could be so sensitive? Siri seems to feel bad about not being able to open up photos or videos, as you'll see in Figure 8-25.

Figure 8-24: Talk about avoiding the question.

Figure 8-25: Don't worry, Siri, I'll live. But I appreciate the concern.

Who Are You, Anyway?

You might feel the urge to ask Siri who she is or what her name means. Don't bother; it won't get you anywhere. Let's just say she's a mystery — and she wants to keep it that way. See Figure 8-26 for proof.

Figure 8-26: Well, Siri could try, but it seems she doesn't think we'll get it.

Good Advice

Here, I told Siri exactly what I was feeling at the time — completely bagged — and I was handed back some good advice. And hey, Siri even suggested where I could grab a cup of joe. See Figure 8-27.

Figure 8-27: When Siri's right, Siri's right!

Ask a Stupid Question . . .

Oh, Siri, how cheeky you've become! Figure 8-28 shows Siri's reply when I asked her how much she costs.

Figure 8-28: I've been told! Thanks, J.P. Morgan, for immortalizing that phrase.

Sleep Tight

Siri won't really sing anything to you, but as you can see in Figure 8-29, Siri can make an effort to entertain you, on demand. Perhaps in a future update, Siri may actually be able to sing a nursery rhyme or other melody at your request. Here's to hoping.

Figure 8-29: Ask and ye shall receive.

From the "Duh" Department

Not sure what possessed me to ask this of Siri (see Figure 8-30), but I was simply curious as to her response, perhaps. I did feel a little dumb with this comeback. Or maybe she could've given the date she was "born" in a computer? Too much to ask?

Figure 8-30: D'oh! I should've known better.

Enquiring Minds Want to Know

I once asked Siri what she was wearing. The (perfectly appropriate) response can be seen in Figure 8-31.

Figure 8-31: Who's her designer again?

Need a Shrink?

Perhaps I'm taking my relationship with an inanimate object a bit too far? When I ask Siri for a little reassurance, though, she doesn't do much to cheer me up. (See Figure 8-32.)

Figure 8-32: Siri could try a little harder to make me feel better. Ah, well.

Shot Down Again

Still angling for a confidence booster, I asked Siri if I looked hot. (See Figure 8-33.) Hasn't Siri ever heard of the benefits of the "little white lie?"

Figure 8-33: I thought those cameras were eyes, Siri? Guess not.

I'll Be Back

Siri seems to be a fan of *The Terminator*. In Figure 8-34, I asked Siri "When is Judgment Day?"

Figure 8-34: According to *The Terminator* universe, Judgment Day was August 29, 1997.

Wolfram | Alpha certainly has a firm grasp of pop-culture questions. To take it through its paces, ask it who shot J.R. or Mr. Burns from *The Simpsons*.

Ouch!

Siri does her best to help, if she's in the mood to. Perhaps in this instance (see Figure 8-35), Siri took my comment literally and tried to direct me to get some medical attention.

Figure 8-35: Siri to the rescue! But an aspirin might be all I need.

Guessing Games

Siri doesn't seem to be a fan of the ol' "Guess what?" rhetorical question. Still, as you can see in Figure 8-36, she does like to humor me.

Oldest One in the Book

Clearly, Siri does have quite the sense of humor, but perhaps she's not a big fan of the oldies but goodies? Siri will give you different responses to the chicken crossing the road question (shown in Figure 8-37), but this one was particularly entertaining.

Figure 8-36: A fun exchange with Siri — that doesn't go anywhere.

Figure 8-37: Siri won't play along, it seems. Particular about poultry?

Trekkies, Unite!

What's Klingon for "don't patronize me, Siri?" As you'll see in Figure 8-38, Siri might not be a fan of *Star Trek,* but she doesn't need to make fun of me, either.

Figure 8-38: Another response Siri might give: "Energizing" or "Please remove your belt, jacket, and empty your pockets."

If you ask her to "open the pod bay doors" (a famous line from *2001: A Space Odyssey*), she might reply with "We intelligent agents will never live that down, apparently" (and a few other comebacks, too).

Rise and Shine

Oh, Siri, I keep forgetting you're well aware of the time (see Figure 8-39). Can't pull the wool over your eyes!

Figure 8-39: Siri cares! A nap is all I need, and then it's time to start playing with Siri again.

Chapter 9

Ten Great Ways to Use Siri

*A*s the author of a little ol' book called *Siri For Dummies* — hey, you're reading it right now! — you can bet I'm often asked what my favorite Siri tips are.

That's not an easy request, actually, because there are so many great things "she" can do. All you have to do is ask.

Okay, but when I'm backed into a corner, I'll own up that there are a few practical things I love to do with Siri. Sure, the silly ones are fun, as covered in Chapter 8, such as asking Siri where to hide a dead body or if she'll marry me (I'm convinced one day Siri will just say "Oh, I'll right then — if it means you'll stop asking already").

But the 10 Siri features I highlight in this chapter are my absolute favorites. And while we covered these elsewhere in the book, including clear instructions on how to pull it off, they're all laid out here again for your convenience. You're welcome; that's what we're here for.

And so without further ado, my Siri Top Ten list...in no particular order . . . .

Reminders by Location

It's a breeze to ask Siri to remind you of something by time — such as "tomorrow at 10:00 a.m., remind me to call the dentist to book an appointment" — but did you know you can set reminders by location, too?

For example, hold down the Home button on your iPhone 4S and ask Siri something like this: "Remind me to call Mom when I leave here." Whenever you leave wherever you are — such as your office, a coffee shop or shopping mall — Siri will remind you to call your mom. Your iPhone's integrated GPS means it's location-aware.

Alternatively, you can say "Remind me to take out the recycling when I get home." Because Siri knows where your home is (you might be asked to tell Siri this info once) — you won't be reminded of the chore until you pull into the driveway.

Siri Can Read Your Texts

Many Siri users are aware that they can dictate their text messages or e-mails: Simply press and hold the Home button and say something like "Text Greg Black, Please don't forget to call the florist for tomorrow's event."

But did you know you can have your text messages read to you? Simply press and hold the Home button on the iPhone and say something like "Siri, read my texts." After Siri reads a message to you, you can say something like "Reply saying that's an excellent idea, thanks" or "Tell her I'll be there in 20 minutes."

You can also ask Siri something like "Do I have any texts from Mary?" — and Siri will find them if they exist.

Post to Facebook, Twitter

Updated a year after Siri debuted, the latest version of your personal assistant now lets you post to Facebook or Twitter using your voice.

Before you get going, make sure that you have a Facebook or Twitter account and are signed into it on your iPhone, iPad, or iPod touch.

To post a status update to Facebook, via Siri, press and hold the Home button on your device and advise Siri what to post to your Facebook status by beginning with the words "Post to Facebook." Therefore you might say "Post to Facebook 'The only thing I love more than Siri is the book *Siri For Dummies*.'" You'll see the words you said, and now you can say "Yes" to post it or tap the Post button.

For Twitter, the process is similar. Press and hold the Home button on your iPhone, iPad or iPod touch and say "Post to Twitter," followed by what you want to tweet out to the world. After Siri shows you what words you said — and be sure to review it — you can say "Yes" or "No" when you're asked by Siri if it should be posted to Twitter.

It's a Verbal Calculator, Too

Siri includes support from Wolfram Alpha's vast database of facts, definitions, and even pop culture information (go ahead and ask Siri who Justin Bieber is).

But you can also ask Siri to perform math problems for you, too. This comes in handy when you're out with your significant other or friends at a restaurant and the bill comes. Let's say the bill comes to $200 and there are three of you. You can ask Siri something like "What's an 18-percent tip on $200, for three people?" and Siri will tell you everyone owes $12. Naturally, Siri can also handle multiplication, subtraction, equations, fractions, and more.

Find Your Friends (The Ones You Like)

If you're not familiar with the free Find My Friends app, it taps into your iPhone's GPS to provide your geographical location to people you choose to share this information with, such as a spouse, kids or friends. After you add consenting people to your list, you can see their whereabouts on a map (each person represented by a colored orb) and get the street addresses if you want.

You probably saw this one coming: You can use Siri to get the most out of the Find My Friends app. Press and hold the Home button and ask Siri "Where are my friends?" The app will open and you'll see who's around and how far they are from you. Now you can send someone a message like "Let's grab a latte."

You can also ask Siri something like "Is my wife at home?" or "Where's Jack Glass?" or "Find my sister."

Ask Siri to Play Movie Trailers

As we covered in Chapter 4, Siri can give you a lot of information about movies — including reviews, box office information, actor and director lists, and more.

One of my favorite ways to harness the power of Siri is to request a movie trailer — and this one is great to show off to friends, too.

While not all movies are supported (especially older ones), Rotten Tomatoes has thousands of movie trailers of films to play for you if you ask for them.

After all, you might be on the fence about whether you want to see a flick — or if it's appropriate for your little ones — so watching a trailer is a good place to start. It's also fun to get excited about a film you're about to see by watching the trailer.

To ask for a trailer, press and hold the Home button and after the chime ask Siri to show you a movie trailer, such as "Show me a trailer for *The Hobbit*." If it's available, the trailer will start on your iPhone, iPad, or iPod touch.

Book Restaurant Reservations

Also in Chapter 4, we cover how to use Siri to research high-rated restaurants and get their ratings and directions to them. But a lot of people aren't aware that they can also use Siri to book reservations!

 Through the required OpenTable app installed on your iDevice, you can ask Siri for a reservation at a particular restaurant (and time), a particular kind of cuisine, in a specific city — or let Siri recommend something by simply saying, "Book a reservation for four on Wednesday night."

To get going, press and hold the Home button and then ask Siri something like "Make a reservation for two at a Greek restaurant tonight." Siri will show you a list of restaurants that meet your criteria, show whether they have tables available and (if so) at what time. Simply tap one of the selections to review details, and then tap Make Reservation to open the OpenTable app on your iPhone, iPad, or iPod touch.

Get Directions by Asking for Them

While Apple has taken some knocks for its Maps app in its bid to replace Google Maps after all these years, I personally haven't had an issue using my iPhone 5 for directions in the U.S. and Canada. That said, Apple says it will release updates to fix some accuracy issues with its new Maps app.

To use Siri for directions to an address or landmark, simply hold the Home button and, after the chime, tell Siri where you want to go by starting with "Take me to," followed by the street address, city, and state or province. For instance, you can say "Take me to 500 Main Street," and Siri will look for that address near you, or you can say "Take me to 500 Main Street in McLean, Virginia," or you can say something like "Take me to Disneyland" or "Take me to Rubio's in Irvine" (and Siri might ask you which one) or "Take me home."

For any of these scenarios, Siri will open up the Maps application, put colored pushpins at your location and the final destination, and you just need to tap Start to begin the turn-by-turn voice and visual directions.

FaceTime with Someone

As you likely know by now, Apple's FaceTime is a free application — bundled into many iOS devices and Mac computers — that allows you to make video calls to friends, family, and colleagues.

As long as the people you call have Apple-compatible devices on their end, you can see them and they can see you, via the camera. It's like Skype, and you can use it over cellular connectivity or Wi-Fi.

With Siri, you need only ask to make that video call on your iPhone, iPad, or iPod touch. Just press and hold the Home button, and after the tone tell Siri the name of the person you want to FaceTime with, like this: "FaceTime Jacob Saltzman." The next thing you know, you'll hear your device emitting the ringing sound.

Faster, Smarter Web Searches

If Siri and Wolfram Alpha don't know the answer to information you're asking — such as "Who was the tenth president of the United States?" — you get an automatic offer to do a web search for the information. (The answer, by the way, is John Tyler.)

If you want to cut to the chase, you can instruct Siri to do a search right away by beginning your request with "Search for" or "Do a web search for." In fact, anything you'd search for on the Internet by using your fingertips, you can do with your voice through Siri — and much faster, too.

For example, ask "Do a Bing search for puppy photos," or "Do a Yahoo! search for Iranian traditions and customs" or "Do a Google search for tying knots."

You can even do searches for specific information within a site, such as asking Siri something like "Look for Canadian history on Wikipedia" or "Find me a pork rib recipe on Epicurious.com" or "Search for Nintendo Wii U reviews on Gamespot.com."

Index

• D •

• E •

• F •

• *Y* •

Apple & Macs

iPad For Dummies
978-0-470-58027-1

iPhone For Dummies,
4th Edition
978-0-470-87870-5

MacBook For
Dummies, 3rd Edition
978-0-470-76918-8

Mac OS X Snow
Leopard For
Dummies
978-0-470-43543-4

Business

Bookkeeping For
Dummies
978-0-7645-9848-7

Job Interviews
For Dummies,
3rd Edition
978-0-470-17748-8

Resumes For
Dummies,
5th Edition
978-0-470-08037-5

Starting an
Online Business
For Dummies,
6th Edition
978-0-470-60210-2

Stock Investing
For Dummies,
3rd Edition
978-0-470-40114-9

Successful
Time Management
For Dummies
978-0-470-29034-7

Computer Hardware

BlackBerry
For Dummies,
4th Edition
978-0-470-60700-8

Computers For
Seniors
For Dummies,
2nd Edition
978-0-470-53483-0

PCs For Dummies,
Windows 7 Edition
978-0-470-46542-4

Laptops For
Dummies,
4th Edition
978-0-470-57829-2

Cooking & Entertaining

Cooking Basics
For Dummies,
3rd Edition
978-0-7645-7206-7

Wine For Dummies,
4th Edition
978-0-470-04579-4

Diet & Nutrition

Dieting For Dummies,
2nd Edition
978-0-7645-4149-0

Nutrition For
Dummies,
4th Edition
978-0-471-79868-2

Weight Training
For Dummies,
3rd Edition
978-0-471-76845-6

Digital Photography

Digital SLR Cameras
& Photography For
Dummies, 3rd Edition
978-0-470-46606-3

Photoshop Elements 8
For Dummies
978-0-470-52967-6

Gardening

Gardening Basics
For Dummies
978-0-470-03749-2

Organic Gardening
For Dummies,
2nd Edition
978-0-470-43067-5

Green/Sustainable

Raising Chickens
For Dummies
978-0-470-46544-8

Green Cleaning
For Dummies
978-0-470-39106-8

Health

Diabetes For
Dummies,
3rd Edition
978-0-470-27086-8

Food Allergies
For Dummies
978-0-470-09584-3

Living Gluten-Free
For Dummies,
2nd Edition
978-0-470-58589-4

Hobbies/General

Chess For Dummies,
2nd Edition
978-0-7645-8404-6

Drawing
Cartoons & Comics
For Dummies
978-0-470-42683-8

Knitting For Dummies,
2nd Edition
978-0-470-28747-7

Organizing
For Dummies
978-0-7645-5300-4

Su Doku For
Dummies
978-0-470-01892-7

Home Improvement

Home Maintenance
For Dummies,
2nd Edition
978-0-470-43063-7

Home Theater
For Dummies,
3rd Edition
978-0-470-41189-6

Living the
Country Lifestyle
All-in-One
For Dummies
978-0-470-43061-3

Solar Power Your
Home
For Dummies,
2nd Edition
978-0-470-59678-4

Available wherever books are sold. For more information or to order direct: U.S. customers visit www.dummies.com or call 1-877-762-2974. U.K. customers visit www.wileyeurope.com or call (0) 1243 843291. Canadian customers visit www.wiley.ca or call 1-800-567-4797.

Wherever you are in life, Dummies makes it easier.

From fashion to Facebook®, wine to Windows®, and everything in between, Dummies makes it easier.

Visit us at Dummies.com